The Consolations of Philosophy

The Consolations
of
Philosophy

ALAIN DE BOTTON

PANTHEON BOOKS · NEW YORK

All rights reserved under International and Pan-American
Copyright Conventions. Published in the United States by
Pantheon Books, a division of Random House, Inc., New York,
and in Canada by Random House of Canada Limited, Toronto.
Originally published in Great Britain by Hamish Hamilton,
a division of Penguin Books Ltd., London.

Pantheon Books and colophon are registered trademarks of
Random House, Inc.

Permissions acknowledgments appear on pages 256–58.

Library of Congress Cataloging-in-Publication Data

De Botton, Alain.
The consolations of philosophy / Alain de Botton.
p. cm.
ISBN 0-679-44276-6
1. Philosophical counseling. I. Title.
BJ1595.5.D43 2000 101—dc21 99-052188

www.pantheonbooks.com

Printed in the United States of America

First American Edition

2 4 6 8 9 7 5 3 1

Consolation for

I Unpopularity 1

II Not Having Enough Money 43

III Frustration 73

IV Inadequacy 113

V A Broken Heart 169

VI Difficulties 203

I

Consolation for Unpopularity

I

A few years ago, during a bitter New York winter, with an after-noon to spare before catching a flight to London, I found myself in a deserted gallery on the upper level of the Metropolitan Museum of Art. It was brightly lit, and aside from the soothing hum of an under-floor heating system, entirely silent. Having reached a sur-feit of paintings in the Impressionist galleries, I was looking for a sign for the cafeteria – where I hoped to buy a glass of a certain variety of American chocolate milk of which I was at that time extremely fond – when my eye was caught by a canvas which a caption explained had been painted in Paris in the autumn of 1786 by the thirty-eight-year-old Jacques-Louis David.

Socrates, condemned to death by the people of Athens, prepares to drink a cup of hemlock, surrounded by woebegone friends. In the spring of 399 BC, three Athenian citizens had brought legal proceedings against the philosopher. They had accused him of failing to worship the city's gods, of introducing religious novelties and of corrupting the young men of Athens – and such was the severity of their charges, they had called for the death penalty.

Socrates had responded with legendary equanimity. Though afforded an opportunity to renounce his philosophy in court, he had sided with what he believed to be true rather than what he knew would be popular. In Plato's account he had defiantly told the jury:

> So long as I draw breath and have my faculties, I shall never stop practising philosophy and exhorting you and elucidating the truth for everyone that I meet . . . And so gentlemen . . . whether you acquit me or not, you know that I am not going to alter my conduct, not even if I have to die a hundred deaths.

And so he had been led to meet his end in an Athenian jail, his death marking a defining moment in the history of philosophy.

An indication of its significance may be the frequency with which it has been painted. In 1650 the French painter Charles-Alphonse Dufresnoy produced a *Death of Socrates*, now hanging in the Galleria Palatina in Florence (which has no cafeteria).

The eighteenth century witnessed the zenith of interest in Socrates'
death, particularly after Diderot drew attention to its painterly
potential in a passage in his *Treatise on Dramatic Poetry*.

Étienne de Lavallée-Poussin,
c. 1760

Jacques Philippe Joseph de
Saint-Quentin, 1762

Pierre Peyron, 1790

Jacques-Louis David received his commission in the spring of 1786 from Charles-Michel Trudaine de la Sablière, a wealthy member of the Parlement and a gifted Greek scholar. The terms were generous, 6,000 livres upfront, with a further 3,000 on delivery (Louis XVI had paid only 6,000 livres for the larger *Oath of the Horatii*). When the picture was exhibited at the Salon of 1787, it was at once judged the finest of the Socratic ends. Sir Joshua Reynolds thought it 'the most exquisite and admirable effort of art which has appeared since the *Cappella Sistina*, and the *Stanze* of Raphael. The picture would have done honour to Athens in the age of Pericles.'

I bought five postcard Davids in the museum gift-shop and later, flying over the ice fields of Newfoundland (turned a luminous green by a full moon and a cloudless sky), examined one while picking at a pale evening meal left on the table in front of me by a stewardess during a misjudged snooze.

Plato sits at the foot of the bed, a pen and a scroll beside him, silent witness to the injustice of the state. He had been twenty-nine at the time of Socrates' death, but David turned him into an old man, grey-haired and grave. Through the passageway, Socrates' wife, Xanthippe, is escorted from the prison cell by warders. Seven friends are in various stages of lamentation. Socrates' closest companion Crito, seated beside him, gazes at the master with devotion and concern. But the philosopher, bolt upright, with an athlete's torso and biceps, shows neither apprehension nor regret. That a large number of Athenians have denounced him as foolish has not shaken him in his convictions. David had planned to paint Socrates in the act of swallowing poison, but the poet André Chenier suggested that there would be greater dramatic tension if he was shown finishing a philosophical point while at the same time reaching serenely for the hemlock that would end his life, symbolizing both obedience to the laws of Athens and allegiance to his calling. We are witnessing the last edifying moments of a transcendent being.

If the postcard struck me so forcefully, it was perhaps because the behaviour it depicted contrasted so sharply with my own. In conversations, my priority was to be liked, rather than to speak the truth. A desire to please led me to laugh at modest jokes like a parent on the opening night of a school play. With strangers, I adopted the servile manner of a concierge greeting wealthy clients in a hotel – salival enthusiasm born of a morbid, indiscriminate desire for affection. I did not publicly doubt ideas to which the majority was committed. I sought the approval of figures of authority and after encounters with them, worried at length whether they had thought me acceptable. When passing through customs or driving alongside police cars, I harboured a confused wish for the uniformed officials to think well of me.

But the philosopher had not buckled before unpopularity and the condemnation of the state. He had not retracted his thoughts because others had complained. Moreover, his confidence had sprung from a more profound source than hot-headedness or bull-like courage. It had been grounded in philosophy. Philosophy had supplied Socrates with convictions in which he had been able to have rational, as opposed to hysterical, confidence when faced with disapproval.

That night, above the ice lands, such independence of mind was a revelation and an incitement. It promised a counterweight to a supine tendency to follow socially sanctioned practices and ideas. In Socrates' life and death lay an invitation to intelligent scepticism.

And more generally, the subject of which the Greek philosopher was the supreme symbol seemed to offer an invitation to take on a task at once profound and laughable: to become wise through philosophy. In spite of the vast differences between the many thinkers described as philosophers across time (people in actuality so diverse that had they been gathered together at a giant cocktail party, they would not only have had nothing to say to one another,

7

but would most probably have come to blows after a few drinks), it seemed possible to discern a small group of men, separated by centuries, sharing a loose allegiance to a vision of philosophy suggested by the Greek etymology of the word – *philo*, love; *sophia*, wisdom – a group bound by a common interest in saying a few consoling and practical things about the causes of our greatest griefs. It was to these men I would turn.

2

Every society has notions of what one should believe and how one should behave in order to avoid suspicion and unpopularity. Some of these societal conventions are given explicit formulation in a legal code, others are more intuitively held in a vast body of ethical and practical judgements described as 'common sense', which dictates what we should wear, which financial values we should adopt, whom we should esteem, which etiquette we should follow and what domestic life we should lead. To start questioning these conventions would seem bizarre, even aggressive. If common sense is cordoned off from questions, it is because its judgements are deemed plainly too sensible to be the targets of scrutiny.

It would scarcely be acceptable, for example, to ask in the course of an ordinary conversation what our society holds to be the purpose of work.

Or to ask a recently married couple to explain in full the reasons behind their decision.

Or to question holiday-makers in detail about the assumptions behind their trip.

Ancient Greeks had as many common-sense conventions and would have held on to them as tenaciously. One weekend, while browsing in a second-hand bookshop in Bloomsbury, I came upon a series of history books originally intended for children, containing a host of photographs and handsome illustrations. The series included *See Inside an Egyptian Town*, *See Inside a Castle* and a volume I acquired along with an encyclopedia of poisonous plants, *See Inside an Ancient Greek Town*.

There was information on how it had been considered normal to dress in the city states of Greece in the fifth century BC.

The book explained that the Greeks had believed in many gods, gods of love, hunting and war, gods with power over the harvest, fire and sea. Before embarking on any venture they had prayed to them either in a temple or in a small shrine at home, and sacrificed animals in their honour. It had been expensive: Athena cost a cow; Artemis and Aphrodite a goat; Asclepius a hen or cock.

The Greeks had felt sanguine about owning slaves. In the fifth century BC, in Athens alone, there were, at any one time, 80–100,000 slaves, one slave to every three of the free population.

The Greeks had been highly militaristic, too, worshipping courage on the battlefield. To be considered an adequate male, one had to know how to scythe the heads off adversaries. The Athenian soldier ending the career of a Persian (painted on a plate at the time of the Second Persian War) indicated the appropriate behaviour.

Women had been entirely under the thumb of their husbands and fathers. They had taken no part in politics or public life, and had been unable either to inherit property or to own money. They had normally married at thirteen, their husbands chosen for them by their fathers irrespective of emotional compatibility.

None of which would have seemed remarkable to the contemporaries of Socrates. They would have been confounded and angered to be asked exactly why they sacrificed cocks to Asclepius or why men needed to kill to be virtuous. It would have appeared as obtuse as wondering why spring followed winter or why ice was cold.

But it is not only the hostility of others that may prevent us from questioning the status quo. Our will to doubt can be just as powerfully sapped by an internal sense that societal conventions must have a sound basis, even if we are not sure exactly what this may be, because they have been adhered to by a great many people for a long time. It seems implausible that our society could be gravely mistaken in its beliefs and at the same time that we would be alone in noticing the fact. We stifle our doubts and follow the flock because we cannot conceive of ourselves as pioneers of hitherto unknown, difficult truths.

It is for help in overcoming our meekness that we may turn to the philosopher.

3

1. The life

He was born in Athens in 469 BC, his father Sophroniscus was believed to have been a sculptor, his mother Phaenarete a midwife. In his youth, Socrates was a pupil of the philosopher Archelaus, and thereafter practised philosophy without ever writing any of it down. He did not charge for his lessons and so slid into poverty; though he had little concern for material possessions. He wore the same cloak throughout the year and almost always walked barefoot (it was said he had been born to spite shoemakers). By the time of his death he was married and the father of three sons. His wife, Xanthippe, was of notoriously foul temper (when asked why he had married her, he replied that horse-trainers needed to practise on the most spirited animals). He spent much time out of the house, conversing with friends in the public places of Athens. They appreciated his wisdom and sense of humour. Few can have appreciated his looks. He was short, bearded and bald, with a curious rolling gait, and a face variously likened by acquaintances to the head of a crab, a satyr or a grotesque. His nose was flat, his lips large, and his prominent swollen eyes sat beneath a pair of unruly brows.

But his most curious feature was a habit of approaching Athenians of every class, age and occupation and bluntly asking them, without worrying whether they would think him eccentric or infuriating, to explain with precision why they held certain common-sense beliefs and what they took to be the meaning of life – as one surprised general reported:

> Whenever anyone comes face to face with Socrates and has a conversation with him, what invariably happens is that, although he may have started on a completely different subject first, Socrates will keep heading him off as they're talking until he has him trapped into giving an account of his present life-style and the way he has spent his life in the past. And once he has him trapped, Socrates won't let him go before he has well and truly cross-examined him from every angle.

He was helped in his habit by climate and urban planning. Athens was warm for half the year, which increased opportunities for conversing without formal introduction with people outdoors. Activities which in northern lands unfolded behind the mud walls of sombre, smoke-filled huts needed no shelter from the benevolent Attic skies. It was common to linger in the agora, under the colonnades of the Painted Stoa or the Stoa of Zeus Eleutherios, and talk to strangers in the late afternoon, the privileged hours between the practicalities of high noon and the anxieties of night.

The size of the city ensured conviviality. Around 240,000 people lived within Athens and its port. No more than an hour was needed to walk from one end of the city to the other, from Piraeus to Aigeus gate. Inhabitants could feel connected like pupils at a school

or guests at a wedding. It wasn't only fanatics and drunkards who began conversations with strangers in public.

If we refrain from questioning the status quo, it is – aside from the weather and the size of our cities – primarily because we associate what is popular with what is right. The sandalless philosopher raised a plethora of questions to determine whether what was popular happened to make any sense.

2. *The rule of common sense*

Many found the questions maddening. Some teased him. A few would kill him. In *The Clouds*, performed for the first time at the theatre of Dionysus in the spring of 423 BC, Aristophanes offered Athenians a caricature of the philosopher in their midst who refused to accept common sense without investigating its logic at impudent length. The actor playing Socrates appeared on stage in a basket suspended from a crane, for he claimed his mind worked better at high altitude. He was immersed in such important thoughts that he had no time to wash or to perform household tasks, his cloak was therefore malodorous and his home infested with vermin, but at least he could consider life's most vital questions. These included: how many of its own lengths can a flea jump? And do gnats hum through their mouths or their anuses? Though Aristophanes omitted to elaborate on the results of Socrates' questions, the audience must have been left with an adequate sense of their relevance.

Aristophanes was articulating a familiar criticism of intellectuals: that through their questions they drift further from sensible views than those who have never ventured to analyse matters in a systematic way. Dividing the playwright and the philosopher was a contrasting assessment of the adequacy of ordinary explanations. Whereas sane people could in Aristophanes' eyes rest in the know-

ledge that fleas jumped far given their size and that gnats made a
noise from somewhere, Socrates stood accused of a manic suspicion of common sense and of harbouring a perverse hunger for
complicated, inane alternatives.

To which Socrates would have replied that in certain cases,
though perhaps not those involving fleas, common sense might
warrant more profound inquiry. After brief conversations with
many Athenians, popular views on how to lead a good life, views
described as normal and so beyond question by the majority,
revealed surprising inadequacies of which the confident manner of
their proponents had given no indication. Contrary to what
Aristophanes hoped, it seemed that those Socrates
spoke to barely knew what they were talking about.

3. *Two conversations*

One afternoon in Athens, to follow Plato's *Laches*, the philosopher
came upon two esteemed generals, Nicias and Laches. The generals
had fought the Spartan armies in the battles of the Peloponnesian
War, and had earned the respect of the city's elders and the admiration of the young. Both were to die as soldiers: Laches in the battle
of Mantinea in 418 BC, Nicias in the ill-fated expedition to Sicily in
413 BC. No portrait of them survives, though one imagines that in
battle they might have resembled two horsemen on a section of the
Parthenon frieze.

The generals were attached to one common-sense idea. They believed that in order to be courageous, a person had to belong to an army, advance in battle and kill adversaries. But on encountering them under open skies, Socrates felt inclined to ask a few more questions:

SOCRATES: Let's try to say what courage is, Laches.

LACHES: My word, Socrates, that's not difficult! If a man is prepared to stand in the ranks, face up to the enemy and not run away, you can be sure that he's courageous.

But Socrates remembered that at the battle of Plataea in 479 BC, a Greek force under the Spartan regent Pausanias had initially retreated, then courageously defeated the Persian army under Mardonius:

SOCRATES: At the battle of Plataea, so the story goes, the Spartans came up against [the Persians], but weren't willing to stand and fight, and fell back. The Persians broke ranks in pursuit; but then the Spartans wheeled round fighting like cavalry and hence won that part of the battle.

Forced to think again, Laches came forward with a second common-sense idea: that courage was a kind of endurance. But endurance could, Socrates pointed out, be directed towards rash ends. To distinguish true courage from delirium, another element would be required. Laches' companion Nicias, guided by Socrates, proposed that courage would have to involve knowledge, an awareness of good and evil, and could not always be limited to warfare.

In only a brief outdoor conversation, great inadequacies had been discovered in the standard definition of a much-admired Athenian virtue. It had been shown not to take into account the possibility of courage off the battlefield or the importance of knowledge being combined with endurance. The issue might have seemed trifling but its implications were immense. If a general had previously been taught that ordering his army to retreat was cowardly, even when it seemed the only sensible manoeuvre, then the redefinition broadened his options and emboldened him against criticism.

In Plato's *Meno*, Socrates was again in conversation with someone supremely confident of the truth of a common-sense idea. Meno was an imperious aristocrat who was visiting Attica from his native Thessaly and had an idea about the relation of money to virtue. In order to be virtuous, he explained to Socrates, one had to be very rich, and poverty was invariably a personal failing rather than an accident.

We lack a portrait of Meno, too, though on looking through a Greek men's magazine in the lobby of an Athenian hotel, I imagined that he might have borne a resemblance to a man drinking champagne in an illuminated swimming pool.

The virtuous man, Meno confidently informed Socrates, was someone of great wealth who could afford good things. Socrates asked a few more questions:

SOCRATES: By good do you mean such things as health and wealth?

MENO: I include the acquisition of both gold and silver, and of high and honourable office in the state.

SOCRATES: Are these the only kind of good things you recognize?

MENO: Yes, I mean everything of that sort.

SOCRATES: ... Do you add 'just and righteous' to the word 'acquisition', or doesn't it make any difference to you? Do you call it virtue all the same even if they are unjustly acquired?

MENO: Certainly not.

SOCRATES: So it seems that justice or temperance or piety, or some other part of virtue must attach to the acquisition [of gold and silver] ... In fact, lack of gold and silver, if it results from a failure to acquire them ... in circumstances which would have made their acquisition unjust, is itself virtue.

MENO: It looks like it.

SOCRATES: Then to have such goods is no more virtue than to lack them ...

MENO: Your conclusion seems inescapable.

In a few moments, Meno had been shown that money and influence were not in themselves necessary and sufficient features of virtue. Rich people could be admirable, but this depended on how their wealth had been acquired, just as poverty could not by itself reveal anything of the moral worth of an individual. There was no binding reason for a wealthy man to assume that his assets guaranteed his virtue; and no binding reason for a poor one to imagine that his indigence was a sign of depravity.

4. Why others may not know

The topics may have dated, but the underlying moral has not: other people may be wrong, even when they are in important positions, even when they are espousing beliefs held for centuries by vast majorities. And the reason is simple: they have not examined their beliefs logically.

Meno and the generals held unsound ideas because they had absorbed the prevailing norms without testing their logic. To point out the peculiarity of their passivity, Socrates compared living without thinking systematically to practising an activity like pottery or shoemaking without following or even knowing of technical procedures. One would never imagine that a good pot or shoe could result from intuition alone; why then assume that the more complex task of directing one's life could be undertaken without any sustained reflection on premises or goals?

Perhaps because we don't believe that directing our lives is in fact complicated. Certain difficult activities look very difficult from the outside, while other, equally difficult activities look very easy. Arriving at sound views on how to live falls into the second category, making a pot or a shoe into the first.

Making it was clearly a formidable task. Clay first had to be brought to Athens, usually from a large pit at Cape Kolias 7 miles south of the city, and placed on a wheel, spun at between 50 and 150

rotations per minute, the speed inversely proportional to the diameter of the part being moulded (the narrower the pot, the faster the wheel). Then came sponging, scraping, brushing and handle-making.

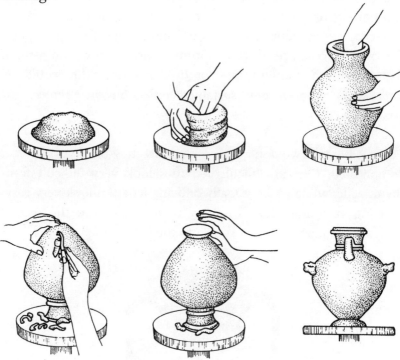

Next, the vase had to be coated with a black glaze made from fine compact clay mixed with potash. Once the glaze was dry, the vase was placed in a kiln, heated to 800 °C with the air vent open. It turned a deep red, the result of clay hardening into ferric oxide (Fe_2O_3). Thereafter, it was fired to 950 °C with the air vent closed and wet leaves added to the kiln for moisture, which turned the body of the vase a greyish black and the glaze a sintered black (magnetite, Fe_3O_4). After a few hours, the air vent was reopened, the leaves raked out and the temperature allowed to drop to 900 °C. While the glaze retained the black of the second firing, the body of the vase returned to the deep red of the first.

It isn't surprising that few Athenians were drawn to spin their own vases without thinking. Pottery looks as difficult as it is. Unfortunately, arriving at good ethical ideas doesn't, belonging instead to a troublesome class of superficially simple but inherently complex activities.

Socrates encourages us not to be unnerved by the confidence of people who fail to respect this complexity and formulate their views without at least as much rigour as a potter. What is declared obvious and 'natural' rarely is so. Recognition of this should teach us to think that the world is more flexible than it seems, for the established views have frequently emerged not through a process of faultless reasoning, but through centuries of intellectual muddle. There may be no good reason for things to be the way they are.

5. *How to think for oneself*

The philosopher does not only help us to conceive that others may be wrong, he offers us a simple method by which we can ourselves determine what is right. Few philosophers have had a more minimal sense of what is needed to begin a thinking life. We do not need years of formal education and a leisured existence. Anyone with a curious and well-ordered mind who seeks to evaluate a common-sense belief can start a conversation with a friend in a city street and, by following a Socratic method, may arrive at one or two ground-breaking ideas in under half an hour.

Socrates' method of examining common sense is observable in all Plato's early and middle dialogues and, because it follows consistent steps, may without injustice be presented in the language of a recipe book or manual, and applied to any belief one is asked to accept or feels inclined to rebel against. The correctness of a statement cannot, the method suggests, be determined by whether it is held by a majority or has been believed for a long time by important people. A correct statement is one incapable of being rationally contradicted. A statement is true if it cannot be disproved. If it can, however many believe it, however grand they may be, it must be false and we are right to doubt it.

The Socratic method for thinking

1. Locate a statement confidently described as common sense.

   Acting courageously involves not retreating in battle.

   Being virtuous requires money.

2. Imagine for a moment that, despite the confidence of the person proposing it, the statement is false. Search for situations or contexts where the statement would not be true.

   Could one ever be courageous and yet retreat in battle?
   Could one ever stay firm in battle and yet not be courageous?

   Could one ever have money and not be virtuous?
   Could one ever have no money and be virtuous?

3. If an exception is found, the definition must be false or at least imprecise.

   It is possible to be courageous and retreat.
   It is possible to stay firm in battle yet not be courageous.

   It is possible to have money and be a crook.
   It is possible to be poor and virtuous.

4. The initial statement must be nuanced to take the exception into account.

Acting courageously can involve both retreat and advance in battle.

People who have money can be described as virtuous only if they have acquired it in a virtuous way, and some people with no money can be virtuous when they have lived through situations where it was impossible to be virtuous and make money.

5. If one subsequently finds exceptions to the improved statements, the process should be repeated. The truth, in so far as a human being is able to attain such a thing, lies in a statement which it seems impossible to disprove. It is by finding out what something is not that one comes closest to understanding what it is.

6. The product of thought is, whatever Aristophanes insinuated, superior to the product of intuition.

It may of course be possible to arrive at truths without philosophizing. Without following a Socratic method, we may realize that people with no money may be called virtuous if they have lived through situations in which it was impossible to be virtuous and make money, or that acting courageously can involve retreat in battle. But we risk not knowing how to respond to people who don't agree with us, unless we have first thought through the objections to our position logically. We may be silenced by impressive figures who tell us forcefully that money is essential to virtue and that only effeminates retreat in battle. Lacking counterarguments to lend us strength (the battle of Plataea and enrichment in a corrupt society), we will have to propose limply or petulantly that we feel we are right, without being able to explain why.

Socrates described a correct belief held without an awareness of how to respond rationally to objections as *true opinion*, and contrasted it unfavourably with *knowledge*, which involved understanding not only why something was true, but also why its alternatives were false. He likened the two versions of the truth to beautiful works by the great sculptor Daedalus. A truth produced by intuition was like a statue set down without support on an outdoor plinth.

A strong wind could at any time knock it over. But a truth supported by reasons and an awareness of counterarguments was like a statue anchored to the ground by tethering cables.

Socrates' method of thinking promised us a way to develop opinions in which we could, even if confronted with a storm, feel veritable confidence.

4

In his seventieth year, Socrates ran into a hurricane. Three Athenians – the poet Meletus, the politician Anytus and the orator Lycon – decided that he was a strange and evil man. They claimed that he had failed to worship the city's gods, had corrupted the social fabric of Athens and had turned young men against their fathers. They believed it was right that he should be silenced, and perhaps even killed.

The city of Athens had established procedures for distinguishing right from wrong. On the south side of the agora stood the Court of the Heliasts, a large building with wooden benches for a jury at one end, and a prosecution and defendant's platform at the other. Trials began with a speech from the prosecution, followed by a speech from the defence. Then a jury numbering between 200 and 2,500 people would indicate where the truth lay by a ballot or a show of hands. This method of deciding right from wrong by counting the number of people in favour of a proposition was used throughout Athenian political and legal life. Two or three times a month, all male citizens, some 30,000, were invited to gather on Pnyx hill south-west of the agora to decide on important questions of state by a show of hands. For the city, the opinion of the majority had been equated with the truth.

There were 500 citizens in the jury on the day of Socrates' trial. The prosecution began by asking them to consider that the philosopher standing before them was a dishonest man. He had inquired into things below the earth and in the sky, he was a heretic, he had resorted to shifty rhetorical devices to make weaker arguments defeat stronger ones, and he had been a vicious influence on the young, intentionally corrupting them through his conversations.

Socrates tried to answer the charges. He explained that he had never held theories about the heavens nor investigated things below the earth, he was not a heretic and very much believed in divine activity; he had never corrupted the youth of Athens – it was just that some young men with wealthy fathers and plenty of free time had imitated his questioning method, and annoyed important people by showing them up as know-nothings. If he had corrupted anyone, it could only have been unintentionally, for there was no point in wilfully exerting a bad influence on companions, because one risked being harmed by them in turn. And if he had corrupted people only unintentionally, then the correct procedure was a quiet word to set him straight, not a court case.

He admitted that he had led what might seem a peculiar life:

> I have neglected the things that concern most people – making money, managing an estate, gaining military or civic honours, or other positions of power, or joining political clubs and parties which have formed in our cities.

However, his pursuit of philosophy had been motivated by a simple desire to improve the lives of Athenians:

> I tried to persuade each of you not to think more of practical advantages than of his mental and moral well-being.

Such was his commitment to philosophy, he explained, that he was unable to give up the activity even if the jury made it the condition for his acquittal:

> I shall go on saying in my usual way, 'My very good friend, you are an Athenian and belong to a city which is the greatest and most famous in the world for its wisdom and strength. Are you not ashamed that you give your attention to acquiring as much money as possible, and similarly with reputation and honour, and give no attention or thought to truth and understanding and the perfection of your soul?' And should any of you dispute that, and profess that he does care about such things, I won't let him go straight away nor leave

him, but will question and examine and put him to the test . . . I shall do this to everyone I meet, young or old, foreigner or fellow-citizen.

It was the turn of the jury of 500 to make up their minds. After brief deliberation 220 decided Socrates wasn't guilty; 280 that he was. The philosopher responded wryly: 'I didn't think the margin would be so narrow.' But he did not lose confidence; there was no hesitation or alarm; he maintained faith in a philosophical project that had been declared conclusively misconceived by a majority 56 per cent of his audience.

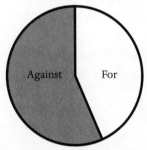

If we cannot match such composure, if we are prone to burst into tears after only a few harsh words about our character or achievements, it may be because the approval of others forms an essential part of our capacity to believe that we are right. We feel justified in taking unpopularity seriously not only for pragmatic reasons, for reasons of promotion or survival, but more importantly because being jeered at can seem an unequivocal sign that we have gone astray.

Socrates would naturally have conceded that there are times when we are in the wrong and should be made to doubt our views, but he would have added a vital detail to alter our sense of truth's relation to unpopularity: errors in our thought and way of life can at no point and in no way ever be proven simply by the fact that we have run into opposition.

What should worry us is not the number of people who oppose us, but how good their reasons are for doing so. We should therefore divert our attention away from the presence of unpopularity to the explanations for it. It may be frightening to hear that a high proportion of a community holds us to be wrong, but before abandoning our position, we should consider the method by which their conclusions have been reached. It is the soundness of their method of thinking that should determine the weight we give to their disapproval.

We seem afflicted by the opposite tendency: to listen to everyone, to be upset by every unkind word and sarcastic observation. We fail to ask ourselves the cardinal and most consoling question: on what basis has this dark censure been made? We treat with equal seriousness the objections of the critic who has thought rigorously and honestly and those of the critic who has acted out of misanthropy and envy.

We should take time to look behind the criticism. As Socrates had learned, the thinking at its basis, though carefully disguised, may be badly awry. Under the influence of passing moods, our critics may have fumbled towards conclusions. They may have acted from impulse and prejudice, and used their status to ennoble their hunches. They may have built up their thoughts like inebriated amateur potters.

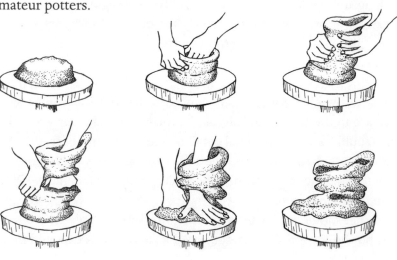

Unfortunately, unlike in pottery, it is initially extremely hard to tell a good product of thought from a poor one. It isn't difficult to identify the pot made by the inebriated craftsman and the one by the sober colleague.

It is harder immediately to identify the superior definition.

ἡ φρόνιμος καρτερία
ἔστιν ἀνδρεία.
Courage is intelligent
endurance.

ἀνδρεῖός ἐστι ὃς ἂν ἐν τῇ τάξει
μένων μάχηται τοῖς πολεμίοις.
The man who stands in the ranks
and fights the enemy is
courageous.

A bad thought delivered authoritatively, though without evidence of how it was put together, can for a time carry all the weight of a sound one. But we acquire a misplaced respect for others when we concentrate solely on their conclusions – which is why Socrates urged us to dwell on the logic they used to reach them. Even if we cannot escape the consequences of opposition, we will at least be spared the debilitating sense of standing in error.

The idea had first emerged some time before the trial, during a conversation between Socrates and Polus, a well-known teacher of rhetoric visiting Athens from Sicily. Polus had some chilling political views, of whose truth he wished ardently to convince Socrates. The teacher argued that there was at heart no happier life for a human being than to be a dictator, for dictatorship enabled one to act as one pleased, to throw enemies in prison, confiscate their property and execute them.

Socrates listened politely, then answered with a series of logical arguments attempting to show that happiness lay in doing good. But Polus dug in his heels and affirmed his position by pointing out that dictators were often revered by huge numbers of people. He mentioned Archelaus, the king of Macedon, who had murdered his uncle, his cousin and a seven-year-old legitimate heir and yet continued to enjoy great public support in Athens. The number of people who liked Archelaus was a sign, concluded Polus, that his theory on dictatorship was correct.

Socrates courteously admitted that it might be very easy to find people who liked Archelaus, and harder to find anyone to support the view that doing good brought one happiness: 'If you feel like calling witnesses to claim that what I'm saying is wrong, you can count on your position being supported by almost everyone in Athens,' explained Socrates, 'whether they were born and bred here or elsewhere.'

> You'd have the support of Nicias the son of Niceratus, if you wanted, along with his brothers, who between them have a whole row of tripods standing in the precinct of Dionysus. You'd have the support of Aristocrates the son of Scellius as well . . . You could call on the whole of Pericles' household, if you felt like it, or any other Athenian family you care to choose.

But what Socrates zealously denied was that this widespread support for Polus's argument could on its own in any way prove it correct:

> The trouble is, Polus, you're trying to use on me the kind of rhetorical refutation which people in lawcourts think is successful. There too people think they're proving the other side wrong if they produce a large number of eminent witnesses in support of the points they're making, when their opponent can only come up with a single witness or none at all. But this kind of reputation is completely worthless in the context of the truth, since it's perfectly

possible for someone to be defeated in court by a horde of witnesses who have no more than apparent respectability and who all happen to testify against him.

True respectability stems not from the will of the majority but from proper reasoning. When we are making vases, we should listen to the advice of those who know about turning glaze into Fe_3O_4 at 800°C; when we are making a ship, it is the verdict of those who construct triremes that should worry us; and when we are considering ethical matters – how to be happy and courageous and just and good – we should not be intimidated by bad thinking, even if it issues from the lips of teachers of rhetoric, mighty generals and well-dressed aristocrats from Thessaly.

It sounded élitist, and it was. Not everyone is worth listening to. Yet Socrates' élitism had no trace of snobbery or prejudice. He might have discriminated in the views he attended to, but the discrimination operated not on the basis of class or money, nor on the basis of military record or nationality, but on the basis of reason, which was – as he stressed – a faculty accessible to all.

To follow the Socratic example we should, when faced with criticism, behave like athletes training for the Olympic games. Information on sport was further supplied by *See Inside an Ancient Greek Town*.

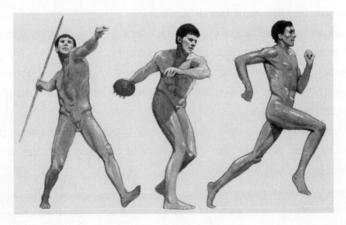

Imagine we're athletes. Our trainer has suggested an exercise to strengthen our calves for the javelin. It requires us to stand on one leg and lift weights. It looks peculiar to outsiders, who mock and complain that we are throwing away our chances of success. In the baths, we overhear a man explain to another that we are ἡμῖν μέλει μᾶλλον τὸ τά σκέλη καλὰ ἐπιδεικνύναι ἢ τὸ βοηθεῖν τῇ πόλει πρὸς τὴν ὀλυμπιονίκην. (More interested in showing off a set of calf muscles than helping the city win the games.) Cruel, but no grounds for alarm if we listen to Socrates in conversation with his friend Crito:

SOCRATES: When a man is . . . taking [his training] seriously, does he pay attention to all praise and criticism and opinion indiscriminately, or only when it comes from the one qualified person, the actual doctor or trainer?

CRITO: Only when it comes from the one qualified person.

SOCRATES: Then he should be afraid of the criticism and welcome the praise of the one qualified person, but not those of the general public.

CRITO: Obviously.

SOCRATES: He ought to regulate his actions and exercises and eating and drinking by the judgement of his instructor, who has expert knowledge, not by the opinions of the rest of the public.

The value of criticism will depend on the thought processes of critics, not on their number or rank:

Don't you think it a good principle that one shouldn't respect all human opinions, but only some and not others . . . that one should respect the good ones, but not the bad ones? . . . And good ones are those of people with understanding, whereas bad ones are those of people without it . . .

So my good friend, we shouldn't care all that much about what the populace will say of us, but about what the expert on matters of justice and injustice will say.

The jurors on the benches of the Court of the Heliasts were no experts. They included an unusual number of the old and the war-wounded, who looked to jury work as an easy source of additional income. The salary was three obols a day, less than a manual labourer's, but helpful if one was sixty-three and bored at home. The only qualifications were citizenship, a sound mind and an absence of debts – though soundness of mind was not judged by Socratic criteria, more the ability to walk in a straight line and produce one's name when asked. Members of the jury fell asleep during trials, rarely had experience of similar cases or relevant laws, and were given no guidance on how to reach verdicts.

Socrates' own jury had arrived with violent prejudices. They had been influenced by Aristophanes' caricature of Socrates, and felt that the philosopher had played a role in the disasters that had befallen the once-mighty city at the end of the century. The Peloponnesian War had finished in catastrophe, a Spartan–Persian alliance had brought Athens to her knees, the city had been blockaded, her fleet destroyed and her empire dismembered. Plagues had broken out in poorer districts, and democracy had been suppressed by a dictatorship guilty of executing a thousand citizens. For Socrates' enemies, it was more than coincidence that many of the dictators had once spent time with the philosopher. Critias and Charmides had discussed ethical matters with Socrates, and it seemed all they had acquired as a result was a lust for murder.

What could have accounted for Athens's spectacular fall from grace? Why had the greatest city in Hellas, which seventy-five years before had defeated the Persians on land at Plataea and at sea at Mycale, been forced to endure a succession of humiliations? The man in the dirty cloak who wandered the streets asking the obvious seemed one ready, entirely flawed explanation.

Socrates understood that he had no chance. He lacked even the time to make a case. Defendants had only minutes to address a jury, until the water had run from one jar to another in the court clock:

35

I am convinced that I never wronged anyone intentionally, but I cannot convince you of this, because we have so little time for discussion. If it was your practice, as it is with other nations, to give not one day but several to the hearing of capital trials, I believe that you might have been convinced; but under present conditions it is not so easy to dispose of grave allegations in a short space of time.

An Athenian courtroom was no forum for the discovery of the truth. It was a rapid encounter with a collection of the aged and one-legged who had not submitted their beliefs to rational examination and were waiting for the water to run from one jar to the other.

It must have been difficult to hold this in mind, it must have required the kind of strength accrued during years in conversation with ordinary Athenians: *the strength, under certain circumstances, not to take the views of others seriously.* Socrates was not wilful, he did not dismiss these views out of misanthropy, which would have contravened his faith in the potential for rationality in every human being. But he had been up at dawn for most of his life talking to Athenians; he knew how their minds worked and had seen that unfortunately they frequently didn't, even if he hoped they would some day. He had observed their tendency to take positions on a whim and to follow accepted opinions without questioning them. It wasn't arrogance to keep this before him at a moment of supreme opposition.

He possessed the self-belief of a rational man who understands that his enemies are liable not to be thinking properly, even if he is far from claiming that his own thoughts are invariably sound. Their disapproval could kill him; it did not have to make him wrong.

Of course, he might have renounced his philosophy and saved his life. Even after he had been found guilty, he could have escaped the death penalty, but wasted the opportunity through intransigence. We should not look to Socrates for advice on escaping a death sentence; we should look to him as an extreme example of how to maintain confidence in an intelligent position which has met with illogical opposition.

The philosopher's speech rose to an emotional finale:

If you put me to death, you will not easily find anyone to take my place. The fact is, if I may put the point in a somewhat comical way, that I have been literally attached by God to our city, as though it were a large thoroughbred horse which because of its great size is inclined to be lazy and needs the stimulation of a gadfly ... If you take my advice you will spare my life. I suspect, however, that before long you will awake from your drowsing, and in your annoyance you will take Anytus's advice and finish me off with a single slap; and then you will go on sleeping.

He was not mistaken. When the magistrate called for a second, final verdict, 360 members of the jury voted for the philosopher to be put to death. The jurors went home; the condemned man was escorted to prison.

5

It must have been dark and close, and the sounds coming up from the street would have included jeers from Athenians anticipating the end of the satyr-faced thinker. He would have been killed at once had the sentence not coincided with the annual Athenian mission to Delos, during which, tradition decreed, the city could not put anyone to death. Socrates' good nature attracted the sympathy of the prison warder, who alleviated his last days by allowing him to receive visitors. A stream of them came: Phaedo, Crito, Crito's son Critobulus, Apollodorus, Hermogenes, Epigenes, Aeschines, Antisthenes, Ctesippus, Menexenus, Simmias, Cebes, Phaedondas, Euclides and Terpsion. They could not disguise their distress at seeing a man who had only ever displayed great kindness and curiosity towards others waiting to meet his end like a criminal.

Though David's canvas presented Socrates surrounded by devastated friends, we should remember that their devotion stood out in a sea of misunderstanding and hatred.

To counterpoint the mood in the prison cell and introduce variety, Diderot might have urged a few of the many prospective hemlock painters to capture the mood of other Athenians at the idea of Socrates' death – which might have resulted in paintings with titles like *Five Jurors Playing Cards after a Day in Court* or *The Accusers Finishing Dinner and Looking Forward to Bed*. A painter with a taste for pathos could more plainly have chosen to title these scenes *The Death of Socrates*.

When the appointed day came, Socrates was alone in remaining calm. His wife and three children were brought to see him, but Xanthippe's cries were so hysterical, Socrates asked that she be ushered away. His friends were quieter though no less tearful. Even the prison warder, who had seen many go to their deaths, was moved to address an awkward farewell:

'In your time here, I've known you to be the most generous and gentlest and best of men who have ever come to this place . . . You know the message I've come to bring: goodbye, then, and try to bear the inevitable as easily as you can.' And with this he turned away in tears and went off.

Then came the executioner, bearing a cup of crushed hemlock:

When he saw the man Socrates said: 'Well, my friend, you're an expert in these things: what must one do?' 'Simply drink it,' he said, 'and walk about till a heaviness comes over your legs; then lie down, and it will act by itself.' And with this he held out the cup to Socrates. He took it perfectly calmly . . . without a tremor or any change of colour or countenance . . . He pressed the cup to his lips, and drank it off with good humour and without the least distaste. Till then most of us had been able to restrain our tears fairly well [narrated by Phaedo]; but when we saw he was drinking, that he'd actually drunk it, we could do so no longer. In my own case, the tears came pouring out in spite of myself . . . Even before me, Crito had moved away when he was unable to restrain his tears. And Apollodorus, who even earlier had been continuously in tears, now burst forth into such a storm of weeping and grieving, that he made everyone present break down except Socrates himself.

The philosopher implored his companions to calm themselves – 'What a way to behave, my strange friends!' he mocked – then stood up and walked around the prison cell so the poison could take effect. When his legs began to feel heavy, he lay down on his back and the sensation left his feet and legs; as the poison moved upwards and reached his chest, he gradually lost consciousness. His breathing became slow. Once he saw that his best friend's eyes had grown fixed, Crito reached over and closed them:

> And that [said Phaedo] ... was the end of our companion, who was, we can fairly say, of all those of his time whom we knew, the bravest and also the wisest and most upright man.

It is hard not to start crying oneself. Perhaps because Socrates is said to have had a bulbous head and peculiar widely-spaced eyes, the scene of his death made me think of an afternoon on which I had wept while watching a tape of *The Elephant Man*.

It seemed that both men had suffered one of the saddest of fates – to be good and yet judged evil.

We might never have been jeered at for a physical deformity, nor condemned to death for our life's work, but there is something universal in the scenario of being misunderstood of which these stories are tragic, consummate examples. Social life is beset with disparities between others' perceptions of us and our reality. We are accused of stupidity when we are being cautious. Our shyness is taken for arrogance and our desire to please for sycophancy. We struggle to clear up a misunderstanding, but our throat goes dry and the words found are not the ones meant. Bitter enemies are appointed to positions of power over us, and denounce us to others. In the hatred unfairly directed towards an innocent philosopher we recognize an echo of the hurt we ourselves encounter at the hands of those who are either unable or unwilling to do us justice.

But there is redemption in the story, too. Soon after the philosopher's death the mood began to change. Isocrates reported that the audience watching Euripides' *Palamedes* burst into tears when Socrates' name was mentioned; Diodorus said that his accusers were eventually lynched by the people of Athens. Plutarch tells us that the Athenians developed such hatred for the accusers that they refused to bathe with them and ostracized them socially until, in despair, they hanged themselves. Diogenes Laertius recounts that only a short while after Socrates' death the city condemned Meletus to death, banished Anytus and Lycon and erected a costly bronze statue of Socrates crafted by the great Lysippus.

The philosopher had predicted that Athens would eventually see things his way, and it did. Such redemption can be hard to believe in. We forget that time may be needed for prejudices to fall away and envy to recede. The story encourages us to interpret our own unpopularity other than through the mocking eyes of local juries. Socrates was judged by 500 men of limited intelligence who harboured irrational suspicions because Athens had lost the Peloponnesian War and the defendant looked strange. And yet he maintained faith in the judgement of wider courts. Though we inhabit one place at one time, through this example, we may imaginatively project ourselves into other lands and eras which promise to judge us with greater objectivity. We may not convince local juries in time to help ourselves, but we can be consoled by the prospect of posterity's verdict.

Yet there is a danger that Socrates' death will seduce us for the wrong reasons. It may foster a sentimental belief in a secure connection between being hated by the majority and being right. It can seem the destiny of geniuses and saints to suffer early misunder-standing, then to be accorded bronze statues by Lysippus. We may be neither geniuses nor saints. We may simply be privileging the stance of defiance over good reasons for it, childishly trusting that we are never so right as when others tell us we are wrong.

This was not Socrates' intention. It would be as naïve to hold that unpopularity is synonymous with truth as to believe that it is syn-onymous with error. The validity of an idea or action is determined not by whether it is widely believed or widely reviled but by whether it obeys the rules of logic. It is not because an argument is denounced by a majority that it is wrong nor, for those drawn to heroic defiance, that it is right.

The philosopher offered us a way out of two powerful delusions: that we should always or never listen to the dictates of public opinion.

To follow his example, we will best be rewarded if we strive instead to listen always to the dictates of reason.

II

*Consolation for Not Having
Enough Money*

I

Happiness, an acquisition list

1. A neoclassical Georgian house in the centre of London. Chelsea
(Paradise Walk, Markham Square), Kensington (the southern
part of Campden Hill Road, Hornton Street), Holland Park
(Aubrey Road). In appearance, similar to the front elevation of
the Royal Society of Arts designed by the Adam brothers
(1772–4). To catch the pale light of late London afternoons, large
Venetian windows offset by Ionic columns (and an arched tym-
panum with anthemions).

In the first-floor drawing room, a ceiling and a chimney-piece
like Robert Adam's design for the library at Kenwood House.

2. A jet stationed at Farnborough or Biggin Hill (a Dassault Falcon 900c or Gulfstream IV) with avionics for the nervous flyer, ground-proximity warning system, turbulence-detecting radar and CAT II autopilot. On the tail-fin, to replace the standard stripes, a detail from a still life, a fish by Velázquez or three lemons by Sánchez Cotán from the *Fruit and Vegetables* in the Prado.

3. The Villa Orsetti in Marlia near Lucca. From the bedroom, views over water, and the sound of fountains. At the back of the house, a magnolia Delavayi growing along the wall, a terrace for winter, a great tree for summer and a lawn for games. Sheltered gardens indulgent to fig and nectarine. Squares of cypresses, rows of lavender, orange trees and an olive orchard.

4. A library with a large desk, a fireplace and a view on to a garden. Early editions with the comforting smell of old books, pages yellowed and rough to the touch. On top of shelves, busts of great thinkers and astrological globes. Like the design of the library for a house for William III of Holland.

5. A dining room like that at Belton House in Lincolnshire. A long oak table seating twelve. Frequent dinners with the same friends. The conversation intelligent but playful. Always affectionate. A thoughtful chef and considerate staff to remove any administrative difficulties (the chef adept at zucchini pancakes, tagliatelle with white truffles, fish soup, risotto, quail, John Dory and roast chicken). A small drawing room to retire to for tea and chocolates.

6. A bed built into a niche in the wall (like one by Jean-François Blondel in Paris). Starched linen changed every day, cold to the cheek. The bed huge; toes do not touch the end of the bed; one *wallows*. Recessed cabinets for water and biscuits, and another for a television.

7. An immense bathroom with a tub in the middle on a raised platform, made of marble with cobalt-blue seashell designs. Taps that can be operated with the sole of the foot and release water in a broad, gentle stream. A skylight visible from the bath. Heated limestone floors. On the walls, reproductions of the frescos on the precinct of the Temple of Isis in Pompeii.

8. Money sufficient to allow one to live on the interest of the interest.

9. For weekends, a penthouse apartment at the tip of the Ile de la Cité decorated with pieces from the noblest period of French furniture (and the weakest of government), the reign of Louis XVI. A half-moon commode by Grevenich, a console by Saunier, a bonheur-du-jour by Vandercruse-La Croix. Lazy mornings reading *Pariscope* in bed, eating *pain au chocolat* on Sèvres china and chatting about existence with, and occasionally teasing, a reincarnation of Giovanni Bellini's *Madonna* (from the Galleria dell'Accademia in Venice), whose melancholy

expression would belie a dry sense of humour and spontaneity – and who would dress in Agnès B and Max Mara for walks around the Marais.

2

An anomaly among an often pleasure-hating and austere fraternity, there was one philosopher who seemed to understand and want to help. 'I don't know how I shall conceive of the good,' he wrote, 'if I take away the pleasures of taste, if I take away sexual pleasure, if I take away the pleasure of hearing, and if I take away the sweet emotions that are caused by the sight of beautiful forms.'

Epicurus was born in 341 BC on the verdant island of Samos, a few miles off the coast of Western Asia Minor. He took early to philosophy, travelling from the age of fourteen to hear lessons from the Platonist Pamphilus and the atomic philosopher Nausiphanes. But he found he could not agree with much of what they taught and by his late twenties had decided to arrange his thoughts into his own philosophy of life. He was said to have written 300 books on almost everything, including *On Love*, *On Music*, *On Just Dealing*, *On Human Life* (in four books) and *On Nature* (in thirty-seven books), though by a catastrophic series of mishaps, almost all were lost over the centuries, leaving his philosophy to be reconstructed from a few surviving fragments and the testimony of later Epicureans.

What immediately distinguished his philosophy was an emphasis on the importance of sensual pleasure: 'Pleasure is the beginning and the goal of a happy life,' asserted Epicurus, confirming what many had long thought but philosophy had rarely accepted. The philosopher confessed his love of excellent food: 'The beginning and root of every good is the pleasure of the stomach. Even wisdom and culture must be referred to this.' Philosophy properly performed was to be nothing less than a guide to pleasure:

The man who alleges that he is not yet ready for philosophy or that

50

the time for it has passed him by, is like the man who says that he is either too young or too old for happiness.

Few philosophers had ever made such frank admissions of their interest in a pleasurable lifestyle. It shocked many, especially when they heard that Epicurus had attracted the support of some wealthy people, first in Lampsacus in the Dardanelles, and then in Athens, and had used their money to set up a philosophical establishment to promote happiness. The school admitted both men and women, and encouraged them to live and study pleasure together. The idea of what was going on inside the school appeared at once titillating and morally reprehensible.

There were frequent leaks from disgruntled Epicureans detailing activities between lectures. Timocrates, the brother of Epicurus's associate Metrodorus, spread a rumour that Epicurus had to vomit twice a day because he ate so much. And Diotimus the Stoic took the unkind step of publishing fifty lewd letters which he said had been written by Epicurus when he'd been drunk and sexually frenzied.

Despite these criticisms, Epicurus's teachings continued to attract support. They spread across the Mediterranean world; schools for pleasure were founded in Syria, Judaea, Egypt, Italy and Gaul; and the philosophy remained influential for the next 500 years, only gradually to be extinguished by the hostility of forbidding barbarians and Christians during the decline of the Roman Empire in the West. Even then, Epicurus's name entered many languages in adjectival form as a tribute to his interests (*Oxford English Dictionary*: 'Epicurean: devoted to the pursuit of pleasure; hence, luxurious, sensual, gluttonous').

Browsing in a newsagent in London 2,340 years after the philosopher's birth, I came upon copies of *Epicurean Life*, a quarterly magazine with articles on hotels, yachts and restaurants, printed on paper with the sheen of a well-polished apple.

The tenor of Epicurus's interests was further suggested by The Epicurean, a restaurant in a small Worcestershire town, which offered its clientele, seated on high-backed chairs in a hushed dining room, dinners of seared sea scallops and cep risotto with truffles.

3

The consistency of the associations provoked by Epicurus's philosophy throughout the ages, from Diotimus the Stoic to the editors of *Epicurean Life*, testifies to the way in which, once the word 'pleasure' has been mentioned, it seems obvious what is entailed. 'What do I need for a happy life?' is far from a challenging question when money is no object.

Yet 'What do I need for a *healthy* life?' can be more difficult to answer when, for example, we are afflicted by bizarre recurring headaches or an acute throb in the stomach area after evening meals. We know there is a problem; it can be hard to know the solution.

In pain, the mind is prone to consider some strange cures: leeches, bleeding, nettle stews, trepanning. An atrocious pain

pulses in the temples and at the base of the head, as though the whole cranium had been placed in a clamp and tightened. The head feels as if it may soon explode. What seems intuitively most necessary is to let some air into the skull. The sufferer requests that a friend place his head on a table and drill a small hole in the side. He dies hours later of a brain haemorrhage.

If consulting a good doctor is generally thought advisable despite the sombre atmosphere of many surgery waiting rooms, it is because someone who has thought rationally and deeply about how the body works is likely to arrive at better ideas about how to be healthy than someone who has followed a hunch. Medicine presupposes a hierarchy between the confusion the lay person will be in about what is wrong with them, and the more accurate knowledge available to doctors reasoning logically. Doctors are required to compensate for their patients' lack, at times fatal, of bodily self-knowledge.

At the heart of Epicureanism is the thought that we are as bad at intuitively answering 'What will make me happy?' as 'What will make me healthy?' The answer which most rapidly comes to mind is liable to be as faulty. Our souls do not spell out their troubles more clearly than our bodies, and our intuitive diagnoses are rarely any more accurate. Trepanning might serve as a symbol of the difficulties of understanding our psychological as much as our physiological selves.

A man feels dissatisfied. He has trouble rising in the morning and is surly and distracted with his family. Intuitively, he places the blame on his choice of occupation and begins searching for an alternative, despite the high costs of doing so. It was the last time I would turn to *See Inside an Ancient Greek Town*.

a blacksmith; a shoemaker; a fishmonger

Deciding rapidly that he would be happy in the fish business, the man acquires a net and an expensive stall in the market-place. And yet his melancholy does not abate.

We are often, in the words of the Epicurean poet Lucretius, like 'a sick man ignorant of the cause of his malady'.

It is because they understand bodily maladies better than we can that we seek doctors. We should turn to philosophers for the same reason when our soul is unwell – and judge them according to a similar criterion:

> Just as medicine confers no benefit if it does not drive away physical illness, so philosophy is useless if it does not drive away the suffering of the mind.

The task of philosophy was, for Epicurus, to help us interpret our indistinct pulses of distress and desire and thereby save us from mistaken schemes for happiness. We were to cease acting on first impulses, and instead investigate the rationality of our desires according to a method of questioning close to that used by Socrates in evaluating ethical definitions over a hundred years earlier. And by providing what might at times feel like counter-intuitive diagnoses of our ailments, philosophy would – Epicurus promised – guide us to superior cures and true happiness.

Epicurus 341 BC–270 BC

4

Those who had heard the rumours must have been surprised to discover the real tastes of the philosopher of pleasure. There was no grand house. The food was simple, Epicurus drank water rather than wine, and was happy with a dinner of bread, vegetables and a palmful of olives. 'Send me a pot of cheese, so that I may have a feast whenever I like,' he asked a friend. Such were the tastes of a man who had described pleasure as the purpose of life.

He had not meant to deceive. His devotion to pleasure was far greater than even the orgy accusers could have imagined. It was just that after rational analysis, he had come to some striking conclusions about what actually made life pleasurable – and fortunately for those lacking a large income, it seemed that the essential ingredients of pleasure, however elusive, were not very expensive.

Happiness, an Epicurean acquisition list

1. Friendship

On returning to Athens in 306 BC at the age of thirty-five, Epicurus settled on an unusual domestic arrangement. He located a large house a few miles from the centre of Athens, in the Melite district between the market-place and the harbour at Piraeus, and moved in with a group of friends. He was joined by Metrodorus and his sister, the mathematician Polyaenus, Hermarchus, Leonteus and his wife Themista, and a merchant called Idomeneus (who soon married Metrodorus's sister). There was enough space in the house for the friends to have their own quarters, and there were common rooms for meals and conversations.

Epicurus observed that:

Of all the things that wisdom provides to help one live one's entire life in happiness, the greatest by far is the possession of friendship.

Such was his attachment to congenial company, Epicurus recommended that one try never to eat alone:

Before you eat or drink anything, consider carefully who you eat or drink with rather than what you eat or drink: for feeding without a friend is the life of a lion or a wolf.

The household of Epicurus resembled a large family, but there was seemingly no sullenness nor sense of confinement, only sympathy and gentleness.

We don't exist unless there is someone who can see us existing, what we say has no meaning until someone can understand, while to be surrounded by friends is constantly to have our identity confirmed; their knowledge and care for us have the power to pull us from our numbness. In small comments, many of them teasing, they reveal they know our foibles and accept them and so, in turn, accept that we have a place in the world. We can ask them 'Isn't he frightening?' or 'Do you ever feel that . . .?' and be understood, rather than encounter the puzzled 'No, not particularly' – which can make us feel, even when in company, as lonely as polar explorers.

True friends do not evaluate us according to worldly criteria, it is the core self they are interested in; like ideal parents, their love for us remains unaffected by our appearance or position in the social hierarchy, and so we have no qualms in dressing in old clothes and revealing that we have made little money this year. The desire for riches should perhaps not always be understood as a simple hunger for a luxurious life, a more important motive might be the wish to be appreciated and treated nicely. We may seek a fortune for no greater reason than to secure the respect and attention of people who would otherwise look straight through us. Epicurus, discerning our underlying need, recognized that a handful of true friends could deliver the love and respect that even a fortune may not.

2. Freedom

Epicurus and his friends made a second radical innovation. In order not to have to work for people they didn't like and answer to potentially humiliating whims, they removed themselves from employment in the commercial world of Athens ('We must free ourselves from the prison of everyday affairs and politics'), and began what could best have been described as a commune, accepting a simpler way of life in exchange for independence. They would have less money but would never again have to follow the commands of odious superiors.

So they bought a garden near their house, a little outside the old Dipylon gate, and grew a range of vegetables for the kitchen, probably *bliton* (cabbage), *krommyon* (onion) and *kinara* (ancestor of the modern artichoke, of which the bottom was edible but not the scales). Their diet was neither luxurious nor abundant, but it was flavoursome and nutritious. As Epicurus explained to his friend Menoeceus, '[The wise man] chooses not the greatest quantity of food but the most pleasant.'

Simplicity did not affect the friends' sense of status because, by distancing themselves from the values of Athens, they had ceased to judge themselves on a material basis. There was no need to be embarrassed by bare walls, and no benefit in showing off gold. Among a group of friends living outside the political and economic centre of the city, there was – in the financial sense – nothing to prove.

3. Thought

There are few better remedies for anxiety than thought. In writing a problem down or airing it in conversation we let its essential aspects emerge. And by knowing its character, we remove, if not the problem itself, then its secondary, aggravating characteristics: confusion, displacement, surprise.

There was much encouragement to think in the Garden, as Epicurus's community became known. Many of the friends were writers. According to Diogenes Laertius, Metrodorus, for one, wrote twelve works, among them the lost *Way of Wisdom* and *Of Epicurus's Weak Health*. In the common rooms of the house in Melite and in the vegetable garden, there must have been unbroken opportunities to examine problems with people as intelligent as they were sympathetic.

Epicurus was especially concerned that he and his friends learn to analyse their anxieties about money, illness, death and the supernatural. If one thought rationally about mortality, one would, Epicurus argued, realize that there was nothing but oblivion after death, and that 'what is no trouble when it arrives is an idle worry in anticipation.' It was senseless to alarm oneself in advance about a state which one would never experience:

> There is nothing dreadful in life for the man who has truly comprehended that there is nothing terrible in not living.

Sober analysis calmed the mind; it spared Epicurus's friends the furtive glimpses of difficulties that would have haunted them in the unreflective environment beyond the Garden.

∞

Wealth is of course unlikely ever to make anyone miserable. But the crux of Epicurus's argument is that if we have money without friends, freedom and an analysed life, *we will never be truly happy*. And if we have them, but are missing the fortune, *we will never be unhappy*.

To highlight what is essential for happiness and what may, if one is denied prosperity through social injustice or economic turmoil, be forgone without great regrets, Epicurus divided our needs into three categories:

> Of the desires, some are natural and necessary. Others are natural but unnecessary. And there are desires that are neither natural nor necessary.

WHAT IS AND IS NOT ESSENTIAL FOR HAPPINESS

Natural and necessary	Natural but unnecessary	Neither natural nor necessary
Friends	Grand house	Fame
Freedom	Private baths	Power
Thought (about main sources of anxiety: death, illness, poverty, superstition)	Banquets	
	Servants	
	Fish, meat	
Food, shelter, clothes		

Crucially for those unable to make or afraid of losing money, Epicurus's tripartite division suggested that happiness was dependent on some complex psychological goods but relatively independent of material ones, beyond the means required to purchase some warm clothes, somewhere to live and something to eat – a set of priorities designed to provoke thought in those who had equated happiness with the fruition of grand financial schemes, and misery with a modest income.

To plot the Epicurean relation between money and happiness on a graph, money's capacity to deliver happiness is already present in small salaries and will not rise with the largest. We will not cease being happy with greater outlay, but we will not, Epicurus insisted, *surpass* levels of happiness already available to those on a limited income.

RELATION OF HAPPINESS TO MONEY FOR SOMEONE
WITH FRIENDS, FREEDOM, ETC.

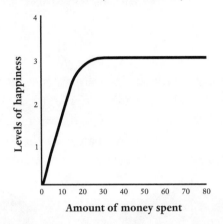

The analysis depended on a particular understanding of happiness. For Epicurus, we are happy if we are not in *active* pain. Because we suffer active pain if we lack nutrients and clothes, we must have enough money to buy them. But suffering is too strong a word to describe what will occur if we are obliged to wear an ordinary cardigan rather than a cashmere one or to eat a sandwich rather than sea scallops. Hence the argument that:

> Plain dishes offer the same pleasure as a luxurious table, when the pain that comes from want is taken away.

Whether we regularly eat meals like the one on the right or like the one on the left cannot be the decisive factor in our state of mind.

As for eating meat, it relieves neither any of our nature's stress nor a desire whose non-satisfaction would give rise to pain . . . What it contributes to is not life's maintenance but variation of pleasures . . . like drinking of exotic wines, all of which our nature is quite capable of doing without.

It may be tempting to attribute this disparagement of luxury to the primitive range of products available to the rich in the undeveloped economy of Hellenistic Greece. Yet the argument may still be defended by pointing to an imbalance in the ratio of price to happiness in products of later ages.

We would not be happy with the vehicle on the left but no friends; with a villa but no freedom; with linen sheets but too much anxiety to sleep. So long as essential non-material needs are unattended, the line on the graph of happiness will remain stubbornly low.

RELATION OF HAPPINESS TO MONEY FOR SOMEONE
WITHOUT FRIENDS, FREEDOM, ETC.

Nothing satisfies the man who is not satisfied with a little.

∽

To avoid acquiring what we do not need or regretting what we cannot afford, we should ask rigorously the moment we desire an expensive object whether we are right to do so. We should undertake a series of thought experiments in which we imagine ourselves projected in time to the moment when our desires have been realized, in order to gauge our likely degree of happiness:

The following method of inquiry must be applied to every desire: What will happen to me if what I long for is accomplished? What will happen if it is not accomplished?

A method which, though no examples of it survive, must have followed at least five steps – which may without injustice be sketched in the language of an instruction manual or recipe book.

1. Identify a project for happiness.

   In order to be happy on holiday, I must live in a villa.

2. Imagine that the project may be false. Look for exceptions to the supposed link between the desired object and happiness. Could one possess the desired object but not be happy? Could one be happy but not have the desired object?

   Could I spend money on a villa and still not be happy?

   Could I be happy on holiday and not spend as much money as on a villa?

3. If an exception is found, the desired object cannot be a necessary and sufficient cause of happiness.

   It is possible to have a miserable time in a villa if, for example, I feel friendless and isolated.

   It is possible for me to be happy in a tent if, for example, I am with someone I love and feel appreciated by.

4. In order to be accurate about producing happiness, the initial
   project must be nuanced to take the exception into account.

   *In so far as I can be happy in an expensive villa, this depends on being
   with someone I love and feel appreciated by.*

   *I can be happy without spending money on a villa, as long as I am
   with someone I love and feel appreciated by.*

5. True needs may now seem very different from the confused
   initial desire.

   *Happiness depends more on the possession of a congenial companion
   than a well-decorated villa.*

*The possession of the greatest riches does not resolve the
agitation of the soul nor give birth to remarkable joy.*

5

Why, then, if expensive things cannot bring us remarkable joy, are we so powerfully drawn to them? Because of an error similar to that of the migraine sufferer who drills a hole in the side of his skull: because expensive objects can feel like plausible solutions to needs we don't understand. Objects mimic in a material dimension what we require in a psychological one. We need to rearrange our minds but are lured towards new shelves. We buy a cashmere cardigan as a substitute for the counsel of friends.

We are not solely to blame for our confusions. Our weak understanding of our needs is aggravated by what Epicurus termed the 'idle opinions' of those around us, which do not reflect the natural hierarchy of our needs, emphasizing luxury and riches, seldom friendship, freedom and thought. The prevalence of idle opinion is no coincidence. It is in the interests of commercial enterprises to skew the hierarchy of our needs, to promote a material vision of the good and downplay an unsaleable one.

And the way we are enticed is through the sly association of superfluous objects with our other, forgotten needs.

It may be a jeep we end up buying, but it was – for Epicurus – freedom we were looking for.

It may be the aperitif we purchase, but it was – for Epicurus – friendship we were after.

It may be fine bathing accoutrements we acquire, but it was – for Epicurus – thought that would have brought us calm.

To counteract the power of luxurious images Epicureans appreciated the importance of advertising.

In the AD 120s, in the central market-place of Oinoanda, a town of 10,000 inhabitants in the south-western corner of Asia Minor, an enormous stone colonnade 80 metres long and nearly 4 metres high was erected and inscribed with Epicurean slogans for the attention of shoppers:

Luxurious foods and drinks . . . in no way produce freedom from harm and a healthy condition in the flesh.

One must regard wealth beyond what is natural as of no more use than water to a container that is full to overflowing.

Real value is generated not by theatres and baths and perfumes and ointments . . . but by natural science.

The wall had been paid for by Diogenes, one of Oinoanda's wealthiest citizens, who had sought, 400 years after Epicurus and his friends had opened the Garden in Athens, to share with his fellow inhabitants the secrets of happiness he had discovered in Epicurus's philosophy. As he explained on one corner of the wall:

Having already reached the sunset of my life (being almost on the verge of departure from the world on account of old age), I wanted, before being overtaken by death, to compose a fine anthem to celebrate the fullness of pleasure and so to help now those who are well-constituted. Now, if only one person, or two or three or four or five or six . . . were in a bad predicament, I should address them individually . . . but as the majority of people suffer from a common disease, as in a plague, with their false notions about things, and as their number is increasing (for in mutual emulation they catch the disease from each other, like sheep) . . . I wished to use this stoa to advertise publicly medicines that bring salvation.

The massive limestone wall contained some 25,000 words advertising all aspects of Epicurus's thought, mentioning the importance of friendship and of the analysis of anxieties. Inhabitants shopping in the boutiques of Oinoanda had been warned in detail that they could expect little happiness from the activity.

Advertising would not be so prevalent if we were not such suggestible creatures. We want things when they are beautifully presented on walls, and lose interest when they are ignored or not well spoken of. Lucretius lamented the way in which what we want is 'chosen by hearsay rather than by the evidence of [our] own senses'.

Unfortunately, there is no shortage of desirable images of luxurious products and costly surroundings, fewer of ordinary settings and individuals. We receive little encouragement to attend to modest gratifications – playing with a child, conversations with a friend, an afternoon in the sun, a clean house, cheese spread across fresh bread ('Send me a pot of cheese, so that I may have a feast whenever I like'). It is not these elements which are celebrated in the pages of *Epicurean Life*.

Art may help to correct the bias. Lucretius lent force to Epicurus's intellectual defence of simplicity by helping us, in superlative Latin verse, to feel the pleasures of inexpensive things:

We find that the requirements of our bodily nature are few indeed, no more than is necessary to banish pain, and also to spread out many pleasures for ourselves. Nature does not periodically seek anything more gratifying than this, not complaining if there are no golden images of youths about the house who are holding flaming torches in their right hands to illuminate banquets that go on long into the night. What does it matter if the hall doesn't sparkle with silver and gleam with gold, and no carved and gilded rafters ring to the music of the lute? Nature doesn't miss these luxuries when people can recline in company on the soft grass by a running stream under the branches of a tall tree and refresh their bodies pleasurably at small expense. Better still if the weather smiles on them, and the season of the year stipples the green grass with flowers.

Ergo corpoream ad naturam pauca videmus
esse opus omnino, quae demant cumque dolorem.
delicias quoque uti multas substernere possint
gratius interdum, neque natura ipsa requirit,
si non aurea sunt iuvenum simulacra per aedes
lampadas igniferas manibus retinentia dextris,
lumina nocturnis epulis ut suppeditentur,
nec domus argento fulget auroque renidet
nec citharae reboant laqueata aurataque templa,
cum tamen inter se prostrati in gramine molli
propter aquae rivum sub ramis arboris altae
non magnis opibus iucunde corpora curant,
praesertim cum tempestas adridet et anni
tempora conspergunt viridantis floribus herbas.

It is hard to measure the effect on commercial activity in the Greco-Roman world of Lucretius's poem. It is hard to know whether shoppers in Oinoanda discovered what they needed and ceased buying what they didn't because of the giant advertisement in their midst. But it is possible that a well-mounted Epicurean advertising campaign would have the power to precipitate global

economic collapse. Because, for Epicurus, most businesses stimulate unnecessary desires in people who fail to understand their true
needs, levels of consumption would be destroyed by greater self-
awareness and appreciation of simplicity. Epicurus would not have
been perturbed:

> When measured by the natural purpose of life, poverty is great
> wealth; limitless wealth, great poverty.

It points us to a choice: on the one hand, societies which stimulate
unnecessary desires but achieve enormous economic strengths as a
result; and on the other, Epicurean societies which would provide
for essential material needs but could never raise living standards
beyond subsistence level. There would be no mighty monuments
in an Epicurean world, no technological advances and little incen-
tive to trade with distant continents. A society in which people
were more limited in their needs would also be one of few
resources. And yet – if we are to believe the philosopher – such a
society would not be unhappy. Lucretius articulated the choice. In
a world without Epicurean values:

> Mankind is perpetually the victim of a pointless and futile martyr-
> dom, fretting life away in fruitless worries through failure to realise
> what limit is set to acquisition and to the growth of genuine pleasure.

But at the same time:

> It is this discontent that has driven life steadily onward, out to the
> high seas . . .

We can imagine Epicurus's response. However impressive our
ventures on to the high seas, the only way to evaluate their merits
is according to the pleasure they inspire:

> It is to pleasure that we have recourse, using the feeling as our
> standard for judging every good.

And because an increase in the wealth of societies seems not to
guarantee an increase in happiness, Epicurus would have suggested
that the needs which expensive goods cater to cannot be those on
which our happiness depends.

6

Happiness, an acquisition list

1. A hut.

2.

3. To avoid superiors, patronization, infighting and competition:

4. Thought.

5. A reincarnation of Giovanni Bellini's *Madonna* (from the Galleria dell'Accademia in Venice), whose melancholy expression would belie a dry sense of humour and spontaneity – and who would dress in manmade fibres from the sales racks of modest department stores.

Happiness may be difficult to attain. The obstacles are not primarily financial.

III

Consolation for Frustration

Thirteen years before painting the *Death of Socrates*, Jacques-Louis David attended to another ancient philosopher who met his end with extraordinary calm, amidst the hysterical tears of friends and family.

The *Death of Seneca*, painted in 1773 by the twenty-five-year-old David, depicted the Stoic philosopher's last moments in a villa outside Rome in April AD 65. A centurion had arrived at the house a few hours before with instructions from the emperor that Seneca should take his own life forthwith. A conspiracy had been discovered to remove the twenty-eight-year-old Nero from the throne, and the emperor, maniacal and unbridled, was seeking indiscriminate revenge. Though there was no evidence to link Seneca to the conspiracy, though he had worked as the imperial tutor for five years and as a loyal aide for a decade, Nero ordered the death for good measure. He had by this point already murdered his half-brother Britannicus, his mother Agrippina and his wife Octavia; he had disposed of a large number of senators and equestrians by feeding them to crocodiles and lions; and he had sung while Rome burned to the ground in the great fire of 64.

When they learned of Nero's command, Seneca's companions blanched and began to weep, but the philosopher, in the account provided by Tacitus and read by David, remained unperturbed, and strived to check their tears and revive their courage:

> Where had their philosophy gone, he asked, and that resolution against impending misfortunes which they had encouraged in each other over so many years? 'Surely nobody was unaware that Nero was cruel!' he added. 'After murdering his mother and brother, it only remained for him to kill his teacher and tutor.'

He turned to his wife Paulina, embraced her tenderly ('very different from his philosophical imperturbability' – Tacitus) and asked her to take consolation in his well-spent life. But she could not countenance an existence without him, and asked to be allowed to cut her veins in turn. Seneca did not deny her wish:

> I will not grudge your setting so fine an example. We can die with equal fortitude, though yours will be the nobler end.

But because the emperor had no desire to increase his reputation for cruelty, when his guards noticed that Paulina had taken a knife to her veins, they seized it against her will and bandaged up her wrists.

Her husband's suicide began to falter. Blood did not flow fast enough from his aged body, even after he had cut the veins in his ankles and behind his knees. So in a self-conscious echo of the death in Athens 464 years previously, Seneca asked his doctor to prepare a cup of hemlock. He had long considered Socrates the exemplar of how one might, through philosophy, rise above external circumstance (and in a letter written a few years before Nero's command, had explained his admiration):

He was much tried at home, whether we think of his wife, a woman of rough manners and shrewish tongue, or of the children ... He lived either in time of war or under tyrants ... but all these measures changed the soul of Socrates so little that they did not even change his features. What wonderful and rare distinction! He maintained this attitude up to the very end ... amid all the disturbances of Fortune, he was undisturbed.

But Seneca's desire to follow the Athenian was in vain. He drank the hemlock and it had no effect. After two fruitless attempts, he finally asked to be placed in a vapour-bath, where he suffocated to death slowly, in torment but with equanimity, undisturbed by the disturbances of Fortune.

David's rococo version of the scene was not the first, nor the finest. Seneca appeared more like a reclining pasha than a dying philosopher. Paulina, thrusting her bared right breast forward, was dressed for grand opera rather than Imperial Rome. Yet David's rendering of the moment fitted, however clumsily, into a lengthy history of admiration for the manner in which the Roman endured his appalling fate.

Loyset Liedet, 1462

Rubens, 1608

Ribera (Jusepe), 1632   Luca Giordano, *c.* 1680

Though his wishes had come into sudden, extreme conflict with reality, Seneca had not succumbed to ordinary frailties; reality's shocking demands had been met with dignity. Through his death, Seneca had helped to create an enduring association, together with other Stoic thinkers, between the very word 'philosophical' and a temperate, self-possessed approach to disaster. He had from the first conceived of philosophy as a discipline to assist human beings in overcoming conflicts between their wishes and reality. As Tacitus had reported, Seneca's response to his weeping companions had been to ask, as though the two were essentially one, where their *philosophy* had gone, and where their resolution against impending misfortunes.

Throughout his life, Seneca had faced and witnessed around him exceptional disasters. Earthquakes had shattered Pompeii; Rome and Lugdunum had burnt to the ground; the people of Rome and her empire had been subjected to Nero, and before him Caligula, or as Suetonius more accurately termed him, 'the Monster', who had 'on one occasion . . . cried angrily, "I wish all you Romans had only one neck!" '

Seneca had suffered personal losses, too. He had trained for a career in politics, but in his early twenties had succumbed to suspected tuberculosis, which had lasted six years and led to suicidal depression. His late entry into politics had coincided with Caligula's rise to power. Even after the Monster's murder in 41, his position had been precarious. A plot by the Empress Messalina had, through no fault of Seneca's, resulted in his disgrace and eight years of exile on the island of Corsica. When he had finally been recalled to Rome, it had been to take on against his will the most fateful job in the imperial administration – tutor to Agrippina's twelve-year-old son, Lucius Domitius Ahenobarbus, who would fifteen years later order him to kill himself in front of his wife and family.

Seneca knew why he had been able to withstand the anxieties:

> I owe my life to [philosophy], and that is the least of my obligations to it.

His experiences had taught him a comprehensive dictionary of frustration, his intellect a series of responses to them. Years of philosophy had prepared him for the catastrophic day Nero's centurion had struck at the villa door.

Double herm of Seneca and Socrates

2

A Senecan dictionary of frustration

Introduction

Though the terrain of frustration may be vast – from a stubbed toe to an untimely death – at the heart of every frustration lies a basic structure: the collision of a wish with an unyielding reality.

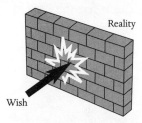

The collisions begin in earliest infancy, with the discovery that the sources of our satisfaction lie beyond our control and that the world does not reliably conform to our desires.

And yet, for Seneca, in so far as we can ever attain wisdom, it is by learning not to aggravate the world's obstinacy through our own responses, through spasms of rage, self-pity, anxiety, bitterness, self-righteousness and paranoia.

A single idea recurs throughout his work: that we best endure those frustrations which we have prepared ourselves for and understand and are hurt most by those we least expected and cannot fathom. Philosophy must reconcile us to the true dimensions of reality, and so spare us, if not frustration itself, then at least its panoply of pernicious accompanying emotions.

Her task is to prepare for our wishes the softest landing possible on the adamantine wall of reality.

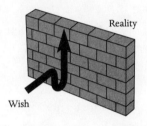

Anger

The ultimate infantile collision. We cannot find the remote control or the keys, the road is blocked, the restaurant full – and so we slam doors, deracinate plants and howl.

1. The philosopher held it to be a kind of madness:

   There is no swifter way to insanity. Many [angry people] . . . call down death on their children, poverty on themselves, ruin on their home, denying that they are angry, just as the mad deny their insanity. Enemies to their closest friends . . . heedless of the law . . . they do everything by force . . . The greatest of ills has seized them, one that surpasses all other vices.

2. In calmer moments, the angry may apologize and explain that they were overwhelmed by a power stronger than themselves, that is, stronger than their reason. 'They', their rational selves, did not mean the insults and regret the shouting; 'they' lost control to darker forces within. The angry hereby appeal to a predominant view of the mind in which the reasoning faculty, the seat of the true self, is depicted as occasionally assaulted by passionate feelings which reason neither identifies with nor can be held responsible for.

   This account runs directly counter to Seneca's view of the mind, according to which anger results not from an uncontrollable eruption of the passions, but from a basic (and correctable) error of reasoning. Reason does not always govern our actions, he conceded: if we are sprinkled with cold water, our body gives us no choice but to shiver; if fingers are flicked over our eyes, we have to blink. But anger does not belong in the category of involuntary physical movement, it can only break out on the back of certain rationally held *ideas*; if we can only change the ideas, we will change our propensity to anger.

3. And in the Senecan view what makes us angry are dangerously optimistic notions about what the world and other people are like.

4. How badly we react to frustration is critically determined by what we think of as normal. We may be frustrated that it is raining, but our familiarity with showers means we are unlikely ever to respond to one with anger. Our frustrations are tempered by what we understand we can expect from the world, by our experience of what it is normal to hope for. We aren't overwhelmed by anger whenever we are denied an object we desire, only when we believe ourselves entitled to obtain it. Our greatest furies spring from events which violate our sense of the ground rules of existence.

5. With money, one could have expected to lead a very comfortable life in Ancient Rome. Many of Seneca's friends had large houses in the capital and villas in the countryside. There were baths, colonnaded gardens, fountains, mosaics, frescos and gilded couches. There were retinues of slaves to prepare the food, look after the children and tend the garden.

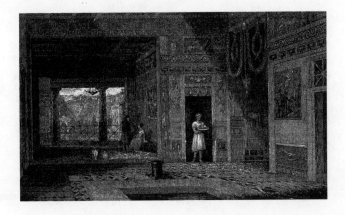

6. Nevertheless, there seemed an unusual level of rage among the privileged. 'Prosperity fosters bad tempers,' wrote Seneca, after observing his wealthy friends ranting around him because life had not turned out as they had hoped.

   Seneca knew of a wealthy man, Vedius Pollio, a friend of the Emperor Augustus, whose slave once dropped a tray of crystal glasses during a party. Vedius hated the sound of breaking glass and grew so furious that he ordered the slave to be thrown into a pool of lampreys.

7. Such rages are never beyond explanation. Vedius Pollio was angry for an identifiable reason: because he believed in a world in which glasses do not get broken at parties. We shout when we can't find the remote control because of an implicit belief in a world in which remote controls do not get mislaid. Rage is caused by a conviction, almost comic in its optimistic origins (however tragic in its effects), that a given frustration has not been written into the contract of life.

8. We should be more careful. Seneca tried to adjust the scale of our expectations so that we would not bellow so loudly when these were dashed:
   When dinner comes a few minutes late:
   What need is there to kick the table over? To smash the goblets? To bang yourself against columns?
   When there's a buzzing sound:
   Why should a fly infuriate you which no one has taken enough

trouble to drive off, or a dog which gets in your way, or a key dropped by a careless servant?

When something disturbs the calm of the dining room:

Why go and fetch the whip in the middle of dinner, just because the slaves are talking?

We must reconcile ourselves to the necessary imperfectibility of existence:

Is it surprising that the wicked should do wicked deeds, or unprecedented that your enemy should harm or your friend annoy you, that your son should fall into error or your servant misbehave?

We will cease to be so angry once we cease to be so hopeful.

Shock

An aeroplane belonging to the Swiss national airline, carrying 229 people, takes off on a scheduled flight from New York to Geneva. Fifty minutes out of Kennedy Airport, as the stewardesses roll their trolleys down the aisles of the McDonald Douglas MD-11, the captain reports smoke in the cockpit. Ten minutes later, the plane disappears off the radar. The gigantic machine, each of its wings 52 metres long, crashes into the placid seas off Halifax, Nova Scotia, killing all on board. Rescue workers speak of the difficulty of identifying what were, only hours before, humans with lives and plans. Briefcases are found floating in the sea.

1. If we do not dwell on the risk of sudden disaster and pay a price for our innocence, it is because reality comprises two cruelly confusing characteristics: on the one hand, continuity and reliability lasting across generations; on the other, unheralded cataclysms. We find ourselves divided between a plausible invitation to assume that tomorrow will be much like today and the possibility that we will meet with an appalling event after which nothing will ever be the same again. It is because we have such powerful incentives to neglect the latter that Seneca invoked a goddess.

2.

She was to be found on the back of many Roman coins, holding a cornucopia in one hand and a rudder in the other. She was beautiful and usually wore a light tunic and a coy smile. Her name was Fortune. She had originated as a fertility goddess, the firstborn of Jupiter, and was honoured with a festival on the 25th of May and with temples throughout Italy, visited by the barren and farmers in search of rain. But gradually her remit had widened, she had become associated with money, advancement, love and health. The cornucopia was a symbol of her power to bestow favours, the rudder a symbol of her more sinister power to change destinies. She could scatter gifts, then with terrifying speed shift the rudder's course, maintaining an imperturbable smile as she watched us choke to death on a fishbone or disappear in a landslide.

3. Because we are injured most by what we do not expect, and because we must expect everything ('There is nothing which Fortune does not dare'), we must, proposed Seneca, hold the possibility of disaster in mind at all times. No one should undertake a journey by car, or walk down the stairs, or say goodbye to a friend, without an awareness, which Seneca would have wished to be neither gruesome nor unnecessarily dramatic, of fatal possibilities.

*Nothing ought to be unexpected by us. Our minds should be sent
forward in advance to meet all the problems, and we should consider,
not what is wont to happen, but what can happen.*

4. For evidence of how little is needed for all to come to nought,
we have only to hold up our wrists and study for a moment the
pulses of blood through our fragile, greenish veins:

> What is man? A vessel that the slightest shaking, the slightest toss
> will break . . . A body weak and fragile, naked, in its natural state
> defenceless, dependent upon another's help and exposed to all
> the affronts of Fortune.

5. Lugdunum had been one of the most prosperous Roman settle-
ments in Gaul. At the junction of the Arar and Rhone rivers, it
enjoyed a privileged position as a crossroads of trade and military routes. The city contained elegant baths and theatres and
a government mint. Then in August 64 a spark slipped out of
hand and grew into a fire that spread through the narrow
streets, terrified inhabitants levering themselves from windows
at its approach. Flames licked from house to house and by the
time the sun had risen the whole of Lugdunum, from suburb to
market, from temple to baths, had burnt to cinders. The sur-
vivors were left destitute in only the soot-covered clothes they
stood in, their noble buildings roasted beyond recognition. The

blaze was so rapid, it took longer for news of the disaster to reach Rome than for the city to burn:

> You say: 'I did not think it would happen.' Do you think there is anything that will not happen, when you know that it is possible to happen, when you see that it has already happened . . .?

6. On the fifth of February 62, similar disaster struck the province of Campania. The earth trembled, and large sections of Pompeii collapsed. In the months that followed, many inhabitants decided to leave Campania for other parts of the peninsula. Their move suggested to Seneca that they believed there was somewhere on earth, in Liguria or Calabria, where they might be wholly safe, out of reach of Fortune's will. To which he replied with an argument, persuasive in spite of its geological dubiousness:

> Who promises them better foundations for this or that soil to stand on? All places have the same conditions and if they have not yet had an earthquake, they can none the less have quakes. Perhaps tonight or before tonight, today will split open the spot where you stand securely. How do you know whether conditions will henceforth be better in those places against which Fortune has already exhausted her strength or in those places which are supported on their own ruins? We are mistaken if we believe any part of the world is exempt and safe . . . Nature has not created anything in such a way that it is immobile.

7. At the time of Caligula's accession to the throne, away from high politics in a household in Rome, a mother lost her son. Metilius had been short of his twenty-fifth birthday and a young man of exceptional promise. He had been close to his mother Marcia, and his death devastated her. She withdrew from social life and sank into mourning. Her friends watched with compassion and hoped for a day when she would regain a measure of composure. She didn't. A year passed, then another and a third, and still Marcia came no closer to overcoming her grief.

After three years she was as tearful as she had been on the very day of his funeral. Seneca sent her a letter. He expressed enormous sympathies, but gently continued, 'the question at issue between us [is] whether grief ought to be *deep* or *never-ending.*'

Marcia was rebelling against what seemed like an occurrence at once dreadful and rare – and all the more dreadful because it was rare. Around her were mothers who still had their sons, young men beginning their careers, serving in the army or entering politics. Why had hers been taken from her?

8. The death was unusual and terrible, but it was not – Seneca ventured – abnormal. If Marcia looked beyond a restricted circle, she would come upon a woefully long list of sons whom Fortune had killed. Octavia had lost her son, Livia her son, Cornelia hers; so had Xenophon, Paulus, Lucius Bibulus, Lucius Sulla, Augustus and Scipio. By averting her gaze from early deaths, Marcia had, understandably but perilously, denied them a place in her conception of the normal:

   We never anticipate evils before they actually arrive . . . So many funerals pass our doors, yet we never dwell on death. So many deaths are untimely, yet we make plans for our own infants: how they will don the toga, serve in the army, and succeed to their father's property.

   The children might live, but how ingenuous to believe that they were guaranteed to survive to maturity – even to dinner-time:

   No promise has been given you for this night – no, I have suggested too long a respite – no promise has been given even for this *hour*.

   There is dangerous innocence in the expectation of a future formed on the basis of probability. Any accident to which a human has been subject, however rare, however distant in time, is a possibility we must ready ourselves for.

9. Because Fortune's long benevolent periods risk seducing us into somnolence, Seneca entreated us to spare a little time each day to think of her. We do not know what will happen next: we must expect something. In the early morning, we should undertake what Seneca termed a *praemeditatio*, a meditation in advance, on all the sorrows of mind and body to which the goddess may subsequently subject us.

A SENECAN PRAEMEDITATIO

[The wise] will start each day with the thought . . .
Fortune gives us nothing which we can really own.
Nothing, whether public or private, is stable; the destinies of men, no less than those of cities, are in a whirl.
Whatever structure has been reared by a long sequence of years, at the cost of great toil and through the great kindness of the gods, is scattered and dispersed in a single day. No, he who has said 'a day' has granted too long a postponement to swift misfortune; an hour, an instant of time, suffices for the overthrow of empires.
How often have cities in Asia, how often in Achaia, been laid low by a single shock of earthquake? How many towns in Syria, how many in Macedonia, have been swallowed up? How often has this kind of devastation laid Cyprus in ruins?
We live in the middle of things which have all been destined to die.
Mortal have you been born, to mortals have you given birth.
Reckon on everything, expect everything.

10. The same could naturally have been conveyed in other ways. In more sober philosophical language, one could say that a subject's agency is only one of the causal factors determining events in the course of his or her life. Seneca resorted instead to continual hyperbole:

> Whenever anyone falls at your side or behind you, cry out:
> 'Fortune, you will not deceive me, you will not fall upon me

confident and heedless. I know what you are planning. It is true
that you struck someone else, but you aimed at me.'
(The original ends with a final, more rousing alliteration:

Quotiens aliquis ad latus aut pone tergum ceciderit, exclama:
'Non decipies me, fortuna, nec securum aut neglegentem
opprimes. Scio quid pares; alium quidem percussisti, sed me
petisti.')

11. If most philosophers feel no need to write like this, it is because
they trust that, so long as an argument is logical, the style in
which it is presented to the reader will not determine its
effectiveness. Seneca believed in a different picture of the mind.
Arguments are like eels: however logical, they may slip from
the mind's weak grasp unless fixed there by imagery and style.
We need metaphors to derive a sense of what cannot be seen or
touched, or else we will forget.

The goddess of Fortune, in spite of her unphilosophical,
religious roots, was the perfect image to keep our exposure to
accident continually within our minds, conflating a range of
threats to our security into one ghastly anthropomorphic
enemy.

Sense of injustice

A feeling that the rules of justice have been violated, rules which dictate that if we are honourable, we will be rewarded, and that if we are bad, we will be punished – a sense of justice inculcated in the earliest education of children, and found in most religious texts, for example, in the book of Deuteronomy, which explains that the godly person 'shall be like a tree planted by the rivers of water . . . and whatsoever he doeth shall prosper. The ungodly are not so: but are like chaff which the wind driveth away.'

$$\text{Goodness} \longrightarrow \text{Reward}$$
$$\text{Evil} \longrightarrow \text{Punishment}$$

In cases where one acts correctly but still suffers disaster, one is left bewildered and unable to fit the event into a scheme of justice. The world seems absurd. One alternates between a feeling that one may after all have been bad and this is why one was punished, and the feeling that one truly was not bad and therefore must have fallen victim to a catastrophic failure in the administration of justice. The continuing belief that the world is fundamentally just is implied in the very complaint that there has been an injustice.

1. Justice was not an ideology that had helped Marcia.

2. It had forced her to oscillate between a debilitating feeling that her son Metilius had been taken away from her because she was bad, and at other moments, a feeling of outrage with the world that Metilius had died given that she had always been essentially good.

3. But we cannot always explain our destiny by referring to our moral worth; we may be cursed and blessed without justice behind either. Not everything which happens *to* us occurs with reference to something *about* us.

Metilius hadn't died because his mother was bad, nor was the world unfair because his mother was good and yet he had died. His death was, in Seneca's image, the work of Fortune, and the goddess was no moral judge. She did not evaluate her victims like the god of Deuteronomy and reward them according to merit. She inflicted harm with the moral blindness of a hurricane.

4. Seneca knew in himself the sapping impulse to interpret failures according to a misguided model of justice. Upon the accession of Claudius in early 41, he became a pawn in a plan by the Empress Messalina to rid herself of Caligula's sister, Julia Livilla. The empress accused Julia of having an adulterous affair and falsely named Seneca as her lover. He was in an instant stripped of family, money, friends, reputation and his political career, and sent into exile on the island of Corsica, one of the most desolate parts of Rome's vast empire.

He would have endured periods of self-blame alternating with feelings of bitterness. He would have reproached himself for misreading the political situation with regard to Messalina, and resented the way his loyalty and talents had been rewarded by Claudius.

Both moods were based on a picture of a moral universe

where external circumstances reflected internal qualities. It was a relief from this punitive schema to remember Fortune:

I do not allow [Fortune] to pass sentence upon myself.

Seneca's political failure did not have to be read as retribution for sins, it was no rational punishment meted out after examination of the evidence by an all-seeing Providence in a divine courtroom; it was a cruel but morally meaningless by-product of the machinations of a rancorous Empress. Seneca was not only distancing himself from disgrace. The imperial official he had been had not deserved all the credit for his status either.

The interventions of Fortune, whether kindly or diabolical, introduced a random element into human destinies.

Anxiety

A condition of agitation about an uncertain situation which one both wishes will turn out for the best and fears may turn out for the worst. Typically leaves sufferers unable to derive enjoyment from supposedly pleasurable activities, cultural, sexual or social.

Even in sublime settings the anxious will remain preoccupied by private anticipations of ruin and may prefer to be left alone in a room.

1. The traditional form of comfort is reassurance. One explains to the anxious that their fears are exaggerated and that events are sure to unfold in a desired direction.

2. But reassurance can be the cruellest antidote to anxiety. Our rosy predictions both leave the anxious unprepared for the worst, and unwittingly imply that it would be disastrous if the worst came to pass. Seneca more wisely asks us to consider that bad things probably will occur, but adds that they are unlikely ever to be as bad as we fear.

3. In February 63, Seneca's friend Lucilius, a civil servant working in Sicily, learned of a lawsuit against him which threatened to end his career and disgrace his name for ever. He wrote to Seneca.

'You may expect that I will advise you to picture a happy outcome, and to rest in the allurements of hope,' replied the philosopher, but 'I am going to conduct you to peace of mind through another route' – which culminated in the advice:

> If you wish to put off all worry, assume that what you fear *may* happen is certainly *going* to happen.

Seneca wagered that once we look rationally at what will occur if our desires are not fulfilled, we will almost certainly find that the underlying problems are more modest than the anxieties they have bred. Lucilius had grounds for sadness but not hysteria:

> If you lose this case, can anything more severe happen to you than being sent into exile or led to prison? . . . 'I may become a poor man'; I shall then be one among many. 'I may be exiled'; I shall then regard myself as though I had been born in the place to which I'll be sent. 'They may put me in chains.' What then? Am I free from bonds now?

Prison and exile were bad, but – the linchpin of the argument – not as bad as the desperate Lucilius might have feared before scrutinizing the anxiety.

4. It follows that wealthy individuals fearing the loss of their fortune should never be reassured with remarks about the improbability of their ruin. They should spend a few days in a draughty room on a diet of thin soup and stale bread. Seneca had taken the counsel from one of his favourite philosophers:

   > The great hedonist teacher Epicurus used to observe certain periods during which he would be niggardly in satisfying hunger, with the object of seeing . . . whether it was worth going to much trouble to make the deficit good.

   The wealthy would, Seneca promised, soon come to an important realization:

   > 'Is this really the condition that I feared?' . . . Endure [this poverty] for three or four days at a time, sometimes for more . . . and I assure you . . . you will understand that a man's peace of mind does not depend upon Fortune.

5. Many Romans found it surprising, even ridiculous, to discover that the philosopher proffering such advice lived in considerable luxury himself. By his early forties, Seneca had accumulated enough money through his political career to acquire villas and farms. He ate well, and developed a love of expensive furniture, in particular, citrus-wood tables with ivory legs.

   He resented suggestions that there was something unphilosophical in his behaviour:

   > Stop preventing philosophers from possessing money; no one has condemned wisdom to poverty.

   And with touching pragmatism:

   > I will despise whatever lies in the domain of Fortune, but if a choice is offered, I will choose the better half.

6. It wasn't hypocrisy. Stoicism does not recommend poverty; it recommends that we neither fear nor despise it. It considers wealth to be, in the technical formulation, a *productum*, a preferred thing – neither an essential one nor a crime. Stoics may live with as many gifts of Fortune as the foolish. Their houses can be as grand, their furniture as beautiful. They are identified as wise by only one detail: how they would respond to sudden poverty. They would walk away from the house and the servants without rage or despair.

7. The idea that a wise person should be able to walk away from *all* Fortune's gifts calmly was Stoicism's most extreme, peculiar claim, given that Fortune grants us not only houses and money but also our friends, our family, even our bodies:

   > The wise man can lose nothing. He has everything invested in himself.

   > The wise man is self-sufficient . . . if he loses a hand through disease or war, or if some accident puts out one or both of his eyes, he will be satisfied with what is left.

   Which sounds absurd, unless we refine our notion of what Seneca meant by 'satisfied'. We should not be happy to lose an eye, but life would be possible even if we did so. The right number of eyes and hands is a *productum*. Two examples of the position:

> The wise man will not despise himself even if he has the stature of a dwarf, but he nevertheless wishes to be tall.

> The wise man is self-sufficient in that he *can* do without friends, not that he *desires* to do without them.

8. Seneca's wisdom was more than theoretical. Exiled to Corsica, he found himself abruptly stripped of all luxuries. The island had been a Roman possession since 238 BC, but it had not enjoyed the benefits of civilization. The few Romans on the island rarely settled outside two colonies on the east coast, Aleria and Mariana, and it was unlikely that Seneca was allowed to inhabit them, for he complained of hearing only 'barbaric speech' around him, and was associated with a forbidding building near Luri at the northern tip of the island known since ancient times as 'Seneca's Tower'.

Conditions must have contrasted painfully with life in Rome. But in a letter to his mother, the former wealthy statesman explained that he had managed to accommodate himself to his circumstances, thanks to years of morning premeditations and periods of thin soup:

> Never did I trust Fortune, even when she seemed to be offering peace. All those blessings which she kindly bestowed on me – money, public office, influence – I relegated to a place from which she could take them back without disturbing me. Between them and me, I have kept a wide gap, and so she has merely *taken* them, not *torn* them from me.

Feelings of being mocked by

(i) inanimate objects

A sense that one's wishes are being purposefully frustrated by a pencil which drops off a table or a drawer that refuses to open. The frustration caused by the inanimate object is compounded by a sense that it holds one in contempt. It is acting in a frustrating way in order to signal that it does not share the view of one's intelligence or status to which one is attached and to which others subscribe.

(ii) animate objects

A similarly acute pain arising from the impression that other people are silently ridiculing one's character.

On arrival at a hotel in Sweden I am accompanied to my room by an employee who offers to carry my luggage. 'It will be far too heavy for a man like you,' he smiles, emphasizing 'man' to imply its opposite. He has Nordic blond hair (perhaps a skier, a hunter of elk; in past centuries, a warrior) and a determined expression. 'Monsieur will enjoy the room,' he says. It is unclear why he has called me 'Monsieur', knowing that I have come from London, and the use of 'will' smacks of an order. The suggestion becomes plainly incongruous, and evidence of conspiracy, when the room turns out to suffer from traffic noise, a faulty shower and a broken television.

In otherwise shy, quiet people, feelings of being slyly mocked may boil over into sudden shouting and acts of cruelty – even murder.

1. It is tempting, when we are hurt, to believe that the thing which hurt us *intended* to do so. It is tempting to move from a sentence with clauses connected by 'and' to one with clauses connected by 'in order to'; to move from thinking that 'The pencil fell off the table *and* now I am annoyed' to the view that 'The pencil fell off the table *in order to* annoy me.'

2. Seneca collected examples of such feelings of persecution by inanimate objects. Herodotus's *Histories* provided one. Cyrus,

the king of Persia and the founder of its great empire, owned a beautiful white horse which he always rode into battle. In the spring of 539 BC King Cyrus declared war on the Assyrians in hope of expanding his territory, and set off with a large army for their capital, Babylon, on the banks of the Euphrates river. The march went well, until the army reached the river Gyndes, which flowed down from the Matienian mountains into the Tigris. The Gyndes was known to be perilous even in the summer, and at this time of year was brown and foaming, swollen with the winter rains. The king's generals counselled delay, but Cyrus was not daunted and gave orders for an immediate crossing. Yet as the boats were being readied, Cyrus's horse slipped away unnoticed and attempted to swim across the river. The current seized the beast, toppled it and swept it downstream to its death.

Cyrus was livid. The river had dared to make away with his sacred white horse, the horse of the warrior who had ground Croesus into the dust and terrified the Greeks. He screamed and cursed, and at the height of his fury decided to pay back the Gyndes for its insolence. He vowed to punish the river by making it so weak that a woman would in future be able to cross it without so much as wetting her knees.

Setting aside plans for the expansion of his empire, Cyrus divided his army into two parts, marked out 180 small canals running off from each bank of the river in various directions and ordered his men to start digging, which they did for an entire summer, their morale broken, all hope of a quick defeat of the Assyrians gone. And when they were finished, the once-rapid Gyndes was split into 360 separate channels through which water flowed so languidly that astonished local women could indeed wander across the trickling stream without hoisting their skirts. His anger assuaged, the King of Persia instructed his exhausted army to resume the march to Babylon.

3. Seneca collected similar examples of feelings of persecution at the hands of animate objects. One concerned the Roman governor of Syria, Gnaeus Piso, a brave general but a troubled soul. When a soldier returned from a period of leave without the friend he had set out with and claimed to have no idea where he had gone, Piso judged that the soldier was lying; he had killed his friend, and would have to pay with his life.

   The condemned man swore he hadn't murdered anyone and begged for time for an inquiry to be made, but Piso knew better and had the soldier escorted to his death without delay.

   However, as the centurion in charge was preparing to cut off the soldier's head, the missing companion arrived at the gates of the camp. The army broke into spontaneous applause and the relieved centurion called off the execution.

   Piso took the news less well. Hearing the cheers, he felt them to be mocking his judgement. He grew red and angry, so angry that he summoned his guards and ordered both men to be executed, the soldier who hadn't committed murder and the one who hadn't been murdered. And because he was by this point feeling very persecuted, Piso also sent the centurion off to his death for good measure.

4. The governor of Syria had at once interpreted the applause of his soldiers as a wish to undermine his authority and to question his judgement. Cyrus had at once interpreted the river's manslaughter of his horse as murder.

   Seneca had an explanation for such errors of judgement; it lay with 'a certain abjectness of spirit' in men like Cyrus and Piso. Behind their readiness to anticipate insult lay a fear of deserving ridicule. When we suspect that we are appropriate targets for hurt, it does not take much for us to believe that someone or something is out to hurt us:

   'So and so did not give me an audience today, though he gave it to others'; 'he haughtily repulsed or openly laughed at my

conversation'; 'he did not give me the seat of honour, but placed
me at the foot of the table.'

There may be innocent grounds. He didn't give me an audience
today, because he would prefer to see me next week. It seemed
like he was laughing at me, but it was a facial tic. These are not
the first explanations to come into our minds when we are
abject of spirit.

5. So we must endeavour to surround our initial impressions with
a fireguard and refuse to act at once on their precepts. We must
ask ourselves if someone who has not answered a letter is *necessarily* being tardy to annoy us, and if the missing keys have
necessarily been stolen:

> [The wise do] not put a wrong construction upon everything.

6. And the reason why they are able not to was indirectly
explained by Seneca in a letter to Lucilius, the day he came upon
a sentence in one of the works of the philosopher Hecato:

> I shall tell you what I liked today in [his writings]; it is these
> words: 'What progress, you ask, have I made? *I have begun to be a
> friend to myself.*' That was indeed a great benefit; ... you may be
> sure that such a man is a friend to all mankind.

7. There is an easy way to measure our inner levels of abjectness
and friendliness to ourselves: we should examine how well we
respond to noise. Seneca lived near a gymnasium. The walls
were thin and the racket was continuous. He described the
problem to Lucilius:

> Imagine what a variety of noises reverberates around my ears!
> ... For example, when a strenuous gentleman is exercising
> himself by swinging lead weights, when he is working hard, or
> else pretends to be working hard, I can hear him grunting; and
> whenever he releases his pent-up breath, I can hear him panting
> in wheezy, high-pitched tones. When my attention turns to a less

active type who is happy with an ordinary, inexpensive massage, I can hear the smack of a hand pummelling his shoulders . . . One should add to this the arresting of an occasional reveller or pickpocket, the racket of the man who always likes to hear his own voice in the bathroom . . . the hair-plucker with his shrill, penetrating cry . . . then the cake seller with his varied cries, the sausage man, the confectioner and everyone hawking for the catering shops.

8. Those who are unfriendly with themselves find it hard to imagine that the cake seller is shouting *in order to sell cakes*. The builder on the ground floor of a hotel in Rome (1) may be pretending to repair a wall, but his real intention is to tease the man trying to read a book in a room on the upper level (2).

Abject interpretation: The builder is hammering *in order to* annoy me.
Friendly interpretation: The builder is hammering *and* I am annoyed.

9. To calm us down in noisy streets, we should trust that those making a noise know nothing of us. We should place a fireguard between the noise outside and an internal sense of deserving punishment. We should not import into scenarios where they don't belong pessimistic interpretations of others' motives. Thereafter, noise will never be pleasant, but it will not have to make us furious:

> All outdoors may be bedlam, provided that there is no disturbance within.

3

Of course, there would be few great human achievements if we accepted all frustrations. The motor of our ingenuity is the question 'Does it have to be like this?', from which arise political reforms, scientific developments, improved relationships, better books. The Romans were consummate at refusing frustration. They hated winter cold and developed under-floor heating. They didn't wish to walk on muddy roads and so paved them. In the middle of the first century AD the Roman inhabitants of Nîmes in Provence decided they wanted more water for their city than nature had granted them, and so spent a hundred million sesterces building an extraordinary symbol of human resistance to the status quo. To the north of Nîmes, near Uzès, Roman engineers found a water source strong enough to irrigate the baths and fountains of their city, and drew up plans to divert the water 50 miles through mountains and across valleys in a system of aqueducts and under-

ground pipes. When the engineers confronted the cavernous gorge of the river Gard, they did not despair at nature's obstacle but erected a massive three-tiered aqueduct, 360 metres long and 48 metres high, capable of carrying 35,000 cubic metres of water a day – so that the inhabitants of Nîmes would never be forced to suffer the frustration of a shallow bath.

Unfortunately, the mental faculties which search so assiduously for alternatives are hard to arrest. They continue to play out scenarios of change and progress even when there is no hope of altering reality. To generate the energy required to spur us to action, we are reminded by jolts of discomfort – anxiety, pain, outrage, offence – that reality is not as we would wish it. Yet these jolts have served no purpose if we cannot subsequently effect improvement, if we lose our peace of mind but are unable to divert rivers; which is why, for Seneca, wisdom lies in correctly discerning where we are free to mould reality according to our wishes and where we must accept the unalterable with tranquillity.

The Stoics had another image with which to evoke our condition as creatures at times able to effect change yet always subject to external necessities. We are like dogs who have been tied to an unpredictable cart. Our leash is long enough to give us a degree of leeway, but not long enough to allow us to wander wherever we please.

The metaphor had been formulated by the Stoic philosophers Zeno and Chrysippus and reported by the Roman Bishop Hippolytus:

When a dog is tied to a cart, if it wants to follow, it is pulled *and* follows, making its spontaneous act *coincide with* necessity. But if the dog does not follow, it will be compelled in any case. So it is with men too: even if they don't want to, they will be compelled to follow what is destined.

A dog will naturally hope to go wherever it pleases. But as Zeno and Chrysippus's metaphor implies, if it cannot, then it is better for the animal to be *trotting* behind the cart rather than *dragged and strangled* by it. Though the dog's first impulse may be to fight against the sudden swerve of the cart in an awful direction, his sorrows will only be compounded by his resistance.

As Seneca put it:

> An animal, struggling against the noose, tightens it . . . there is no yoke so tight that it will not hurt the animal less if it pulls *with* it than if it fights *against* it. The one alleviation for overwhelming evils is to endure and bow to necessity.

To reduce the violence of our mutiny against events which veer away from our intentions, we should reflect that we, too, are never without a leash around our neck. The wise will learn to identify what is necessary and follow it at once, rather than exhaust themselves in protest. When a wise man is told that his suitcase has been lost in transit, he will resign himself in seconds to the fact. Seneca reported how the founder of Stoicism had behaved upon the loss of his possessions:

> When Zeno received news of a shipwreck and heard that all his luggage had been sunk, he said, 'Fortune bids me to be a less encumbered philosopher.'

It may sound like a recipe for passivity and quietude, encourage- ment to resign ourselves to frustrations that might have been overcome. It could leave us without heart to build even a dim- inutive aqueduct like that in Bornègre, in a valley a few kilometres north of the Pont du Gard, a modest 17 metres long and 4 metres high.

But Seneca's point is more subtle. It is no less unreasonable to accept something as necessary when it *isn't* as to rebel against something when it *is*. We can as easily go astray by accepting the unnecessary and denying the possible, as by denying the necessary and wishing for the impossible. It is for reason to make the distinction.

Whatever the similarities between ourselves and a dog on a leash, we have a critical advantage: we have reason and the dog doesn't. So the animal does not at first grasp that he is even tied to a leash, nor understand the connection between the swerves of the cart and the pain in his neck. He will be confused by the changes in direc- tion, it will be hard for him to calculate the cart's trajectory, and so he will suffer constant painful jolts. But reason enables us to the- orize with accuracy about the path of our cart, which offers us a chance, unique among living beings, to increase our sense of free- dom by ensuring a good slack between ourselves and necessity. Reason allows us to determine when our wishes are in irrevocable conflict with reality, and then bids us to submit ourselves willingly, rather than angrily or bitterly, to necessities. We may be powerless to alter certain events, but we remain free to choose our attitude towards them, and it is in our spontaneous acceptance of necessity that we find our distinctive freedom.

In February 62, Seneca came up against an unalterable reality. Nero ceased to listen to his old tutor, he shunned his company, encouraged slander of him at court and appointed a bloodthirsty praetorian prefect, Ofonius Tigellinus, to assist him in indulging his taste for random murder and sexual cruelty. Virgins were taken off the streets of Rome and brought to the emperor's chambers. Senators' wives were forced to participate in orgies, and saw their husbands killed in front of them. Nero roamed the city at night disguised as an ordinary citizen and slashed the throats of passers-by in back alleys. He fell in love with a young boy who he wished could have been a girl, and so he castrated him and went through a mock wedding ceremony. Romans wryly joked that their lives would have been more tolerable if Nero's father Domitius had married that sort of a woman. Knowing he was in extreme danger, Seneca attempted to withdraw from court and remain quietly in his villa outside Rome. Twice he offered his resignation; twice Nero refused, embracing him tightly and swearing that he would rather die than harm his beloved tutor. Nothing in Seneca's experience could allow him to believe such promises.

He turned to philosophy. He could not escape Nero, and what he could not change, reason asked him to accept. During what might have been intolerably anxious years, Seneca devoted himself to the study of nature. He began writing a book about the earth and the planets. He looked at the vast sky and the constellation of the heavens, he studied the unbounded sea and the high mountains. He observed flashes of lightning and speculated on their origins:

> A lightning bolt is fire that has been compressed and hurled violently. Sometimes we take up water in our two clasped hands and pressing our palms together squirt out water the way a pump does. Suppose something like this occurs in the clouds. The constricted space of the compressed clouds forces out the air that is between them and by means of this pressure sets the air afire and hurls it the way a catapult does.

He considered earthquakes and decided they were the result of air trapped inside the earth that had sought a way out, a form of geological flatulence:

> Among the arguments that prove earthquakes occur because of

moving air, this is one you shouldn't hesitate to put forward: when a great tremor has exhausted its rage against cities and countries, another equal to it cannot follow. After the largest shock, there are only gentle quakes because the first tremor, acting with greater vehemence, has created an exit for the struggling air.

It hardly mattered that Seneca's science was faulty; it was more significant that a man whose life could at any time have been cut short by the caprice of a murderous emperor appeared to gain immense relief from the spectacle of nature – perhaps because in mighty natural phenomena lie reminders of all that we are powerless to change, of all that we must accept. Glaciers, volcanoes, earthquakes and hurricanes stand as impressive symbols of what exceeds us. In the human world, we grow to believe that we may always alter our destinies, and hope and worry accordingly. It is apparent from the heedless pounding of the oceans or the flight of comets across the night sky that there are forces entirely indifferent to our desires. The indifference is not nature's alone; humans can wield equally blind powers over their fellows, but it is nature which gives us a most elegant lesson in the necessities to which we are subject:

> Winter brings on cold weather; and we must shiver. Summer returns, with its heat; and we must sweat. Unseasonable weather upsets the health; and we must fall ill. In certain places we may meet with wild beasts, or with men who are more destructive than any beasts . . . And we cannot change this order of things . . . it is to this law [of Nature] that our souls must adjust themselves, this they should follow, this they should obey . . . That which you cannot reform, it is best to endure.

Seneca began his book on nature as soon as he had first offered Nero his resignation. He was granted three years. Then in April 65, Piso's plot against the emperor was uncovered, and a centurion dispatched to the philosopher's villa. He was ready. Topless Paulina and her maids might have collapsed into tears –

– but Seneca had learned to follow the cart obediently, and slit his veins without protest. As he had reminded Marcia on the loss of her son Metilius:

> What need is there to weep over parts of life?
> The whole of it calls for tears.

IV

Consolation for Inadequacy

I

After centuries of neglect, at times hostility, after being scattered and burnt and surviving only in partial forms in the vaults and libraries of monasteries, the wisdom of ancient Greece and Rome returned triumphantly to favour in the sixteenth century. Among the intellectual élites of Europe, a consensus emerged that the finest thinking the world had yet known had occurred in the minds of a handful of geniuses in the city states of Greece and the Italian peninsula between the construction of the Parthenon and the sack of Rome – and that there was no greater imperative for the educated than to familiarize themselves with the richness of these works. Major new editions were prepared of, among others, Plato, Lucretius, Seneca, Aristotle, Catullus, Longinus and Cicero, and selections from the classics – Erasmus's *Apophthegmata* and *Adages*, Stobeus's *Sententiae*, Antonio de Guevara's *Golden Epistles* and Petrus Crinitus's *Honorable Learning* – spread into libraries across Europe.

In south-western France, on the summit of a wooded hill 30 miles east of Bordeaux, sat a handsome castle made of yellow stone with dark-red roofs.

It was home to a middle-aged nobleman, his wife Françoise, his daughter Léonor, their staff and their animals (chickens, goats, dogs and horses). Michel de Montaigne's grandfather had bought the property in 1477 from the proceeds of the family salt-fish business, his father had added some wings and extended the land under cultivation, and the son had been looking after it since the age of thirty-five, though he had little interest in household management and knew almost nothing about farming ('I can scarcely tell my cabbages from my lettuces').

He preferred to pass his time in a circular library on the third floor of a tower at one corner of the castle: 'I spend most days of my life there, and most hours of each day.'

The library had three windows (with what Montaigne described as 'splendid and unhampered views'), a desk, a chair and, arranged on five tiers of shelves in a semicircle, about a thousand volumes of philosophy, history, poetry and religion. It was here that Montaigne read Socrates' ('the wisest man that ever was') steadfast address to the impatient jurors of Athens in a Latin edition of Plato translated by Marsilio Ficino; here that he read Epicurus's vision of happiness in Diogenes Laertius's *Lives* and Lucretius's *De Rerum Natura*, edited by Denys Lambin in 1563; and here that he read and re-read Seneca (an author 'strikingly suited to my humour') in a new set of his works printed in Basle in 1557.

He had been initiated in the classics at an early age. He had been taught Latin as a first language. By seven or eight, he had read Ovid's *Metamorphoses*. Before he was sixteen, he had bought a set of Virgil and knew intimately the *Aeneid*, as well as Terence, Plautus and the *Commentaries* of Caesar. And such was his devotion to books that, after working as a counsellor in the Parlement of Bordeaux for thirteen years, he retired with the idea of devoting himself entirely to them. Reading was the solace of his life:

> It consoles me in my retreat; it relieves me of the weight of distressing idleness and, at any time, can rid me of boring company. It blunts the stabs of pain whenever pain is not too overpowering and extreme. To distract me from morose thoughts, I simply need to have recourse to books.

But the library shelves, with their implication of an unbounded admiration for the life of the mind, did not tell the full story. One had to look more closely around the library, stand in the middle of the room and tilt one's head to the ceiling: in the mid-1570s Montaigne had a set of fifty-seven short inscriptions culled from the Bible and the classics painted across the wooden beams, and these suggested some profound reservations about the benefits of having a mind:

The happiest life is to be without thought. – Sophocles
Have you seen a man who thinks he is wise? You have more to
hope for from a madman than from him. – Proverbs
There is nothing certain but uncertainty, nothing more miserable
and more proud than man. – Pliny
Everything is too complicated for men to be able to understand. –
Ecclesiastes

Ancient philosophers had believed that our powers of reason could
afford us a happiness and greatness denied to other creatures.
Reason allowed us to control our passions and to correct the false
notions prompted by our instincts. Reason tempered the wild
demands of our bodies and led us to a balanced relationship with
our appetites for food and sex. Reason was a sophisticated, almost
divine, tool offering us mastery over the world and ourselves.

In the *Tusculan Disputations*, of which there was a copy in the round
library, Cicero had heaped praise upon the benefits of intellectual
work:

> There is no occupation so sweet as scholarship; scholarship is the
> means of making known to us, while still in this world, the infinity
> of matter, the immense grandeur of Nature, the heavens, the lands
> and the seas. Scholarship has taught us piety, moderation, greatness
> of heart; it snatches our souls from darkness and shows them all
> things, the high and the low, the first, the last and everything in
> between; scholarship furnishes us with the means of living well and
> happily; it teaches us how to spend our lives without discontent and
> without vexation.

Though he owned a thousand books and had benefited from a fine
classical education, this laudation so infuriated Montaigne, it ran so
contrary to the spirit of the library beams, that he expressed his
indignation with uncharacteristic ferocity:

> Man is a wretched creature . . . just listen to him bragging . . . Is this
> fellow describing the properties of almighty and everlasting God! In

practice, thousands of little women in their villages have lived more gentle, more equable and more constant lives than [Cicero].

The Roman philosopher had overlooked how violently unhappy most scholars were; he had arrogantly disregarded the appalling troubles for which human beings, alone among all other creatures, had been singled out – troubles which might in dark moments leave us regretting that we had not been born ants or tortoises.

Or goats. I found her in the yard of a farm a few kilometres from Montaigne's château, in the hamlet of Les Gauchers.

She had never read the *Tusculan Disputations* nor Cicero's *On the Laws*. And yet she seemed content, nibbling at stray pieces of lettuce, occasionally shaking her head like an elderly woman expressing quiet disagreement. It was not an unenviable existence.

Montaigne was himself struck by, and elaborated upon the advantages of living as an animal rather than as a reasoning human with a large library. Animals knew instinctively how to help themselves when they were sick: goats could pick out dittany from a thousand other plants if they were wounded, tortoises automatically looked for origanum when they were bitten by vipers, and storks could give themselves salt-water enemas. By contrast, humans were forced to rely on expensive, misguided doctors (medicine chests were filled with absurd prescriptions: 'the urine of a lizard, the droppings of an elephant, the liver of a mole, blood drawn from under the right wing of a white pigeon, and for those of us with colic paroxysms, triturated rat shit').

Animals also instinctively understood complex ideas without suffering long periods of study. Tunny-fish were spontaneous experts in astrology. 'Wherever they may be when they are surprised by the winter solstice, there they remain until the following equinox,' reported Montaigne. They understood geometry and arithmetic, too, for they swam together in groups in the shape of a perfect cube: 'If you count one line of them you have the count of the whole school, since the same figure applies to their depth, breadth and length.' Dogs had an innate grasp of dialectical logic. Montaigne mentioned one who, looking for his master, came upon a three-pronged fork in the road. He first looked down one road, then another, and then ran down the third after concluding that his master must have chosen it:

> Here was pure dialectic: the dog made use of disjunctive and copulative propositions and adequately enumerated the parts. Does it matter whether he learned all this from himself or from the *Dialectica* of George of Trebizond?

Animals frequently had the upper hand in love as well. Montaigne read enviously of an elephant who had fallen in love with a flower-seller in Alexandria. When being led through the market, he knew how to slip his wrinkled trunk through her neckband and would massage her breasts with a dexterity no human could match.

And without trying, the humblest farm animal could exceed the philosophical detachment of the wisest sages of antiquity. The Greek philosopher Pyrrho once travelled on a ship which ran into a fierce storm. All around him passengers began to panic, afraid that the mutinous waves would shatter their fragile craft. But one passenger did not lose his composure and sat quietly in a corner, wearing a tranquil expression. He was a pig:

> Dare we conclude that the benefit of reason (which we praise so highly and on account of which we esteem ourselves to be lords and masters of all creation) was placed in us for our torment? What use is knowledge if, for its sake, we lose the calm and repose which we should enjoy without it and if it makes our condition worse than that of Pyrrho's pig?

It was questionable whether the mind gave us anything to be grateful for:

> We have been allotted inconstancy, hesitation, doubt, pain, super-stition, worries about what will happen (even after we are dead), ambition, greed, jealousy, envy, unruly, insane and untameable appetites, war, lies, disloyalty, backbiting and curiosity. We take pride in our fair, discursive reason and our capacity to judge and to know, but we have bought them at a price which is strangely excessive.

If offered a choice, Montaigne would in the end perhaps not have opted to live as a goat – but only just. Cicero had presented the benevolent picture of reason. Sixteen centuries later, it was for Montaigne to introduce the adverse:

> To learn that we have said or done a stupid thing is nothing, we must learn a more ample and important lesson: *that we are but blockheads*.

– the biggest blockheads of all being philosophers like Cicero who had never suspected they might even be such things. Misplaced confidence in reason was the well-spring of idiocy – and, indirectly, also of inadequacy.

Beneath his painted beams, Montaigne had outlined a new kind of philosophy, one which acknowledged how far we were from the rational, serene creatures whom most of the ancient thinkers had taken us to be. We were for the most part hysterical and demented, gross and agitated souls beside whom animals were in many respects paragons of health and virtue – an unfortunate reality which philosophy was obliged to reflect, but rarely did:

> Our life consists partly in madness, partly in wisdom: whoever writes about it merely respectfully and by rule leaves more than half of it behind.

And yet if we accepted our frailties, and ceased claiming a mastery we did not have, we stood to find – in Montaigne's generous, redemptive philosophy – that we were ultimately still adequate in our own distinctive half-wise, half-blockheadish way.

2

On Sexual Inadequacy

How problematic to have both a body and a mind, for the former stands in almost monstrous contrast to the latter's dignity and intelligence. Our bodies smell, ache, sag, pulse, throb and age. They force us to fart and burp, and to abandon sensible plans in order to lie in bed with people, sweating and letting out intense sounds reminiscent of hyenas calling out to one another across the barren wastes of the American deserts. Our bodies hold our minds hostage to their whims and rhythms. Our whole perspective on life can be altered by the digestion of a heavy lunch. 'I feel quite a different person before and after a meal,' concurred Montaigne:

> When good health and a fine sunny day smile at me, I am quite
> debonair; give me an ingrowing toe-nail, and I am touchy, bad-
> tempered and unapproachable.

Even the greatest philosophers have not been spared bodily humil-iation. 'Imagine Plato struck down by epilepsy or apoplexy,' pro-posed Montaigne, 'then challenge him to get any help from all those noble and splendid faculties of his soul.' Or imagine that in the middle of a symposium, Plato had been struck by a need to fart:

> That sphincter which serves to discharge our stomachs has dilations
> and contractions proper to itself, independent of our wishes or even
> opposed to them.

Montaigne heard of a man who knew how to fart at will, and on occasion arranged a sequence of farts in a metrical accompaniment to poetry, but such mastery did not contravene his general observa-tion that our bodies have the upper hand over our minds, and that the sphincter is 'most indiscreet and disorderly'. Montaigne even heard a tragic case of one behind 'so stormy and churlish that it has obliged its master to fart forth wind constantly and unremittingly for forty years and is thus bringing him to his death.'

No wonder we may be tempted to deny our uncomfortable, insulting coexistence with these vessels. Montaigne met a woman who, acutely aware of how repulsive her digestive organs were, tried to live as though she didn't have any:

> [This] lady (amongst the greatest) . . . shares the opinion that chewing distorts the face, derogating greatly from women's grace and beauty; so when hungry, she avoids appearing in public. And I know a man who cannot tolerate watching people eat nor others watching him do so: he shuns all company even more when he fills his belly than when he empties it.

Montaigne knew men so overwhelmed by their sexual longings that they ended their torment through castration. Others tried to suppress their lust by applying snow-and-vinegar compresses to their overactive testicles. The Emperor Maximilian, conscious of a conflict between being regal and having a body, ordered that no one should see him naked, particularly below the waist. He expressly requested in his will that he be buried in a set of linen underpants. 'He should have added a codicil,' noted Montaigne, 'saying that the man who pulled them on ought to be blindfolded.'

However drawn we may be towards such radical measures, Montaigne's philosophy is one of reconciliation: 'The most uncouth of our afflictions is to despise our being.' Rather than trying to cut ourselves in two, we should cease waging civil war on our perplexing physical envelopes and learn to accept them as unalterable facts of our condition, neither so terrible nor so humiliating.

In the summer of 1993, L. and I travelled to northern Portugal for a holiday. We drove along the villages of the Minho, then spent a few days south of Viana do Castelo. It was here, on the last night of our holiday, in a small hotel overlooking the sea, that I realized – quite without warning – that I could no longer make love. It would hardly have been possible to surmount, let alone mention the experience, if I had not, a few months before going to Portugal, come across the twenty-first chapter of the first volume of Montaigne's *Essays*.

The author recounted therein that a friend of his had heard a man explain how he had lost his erection just as he prepared to enter a woman. The embarrassment of the detumescence struck Montaigne's friend with such force, that the next time he was in bed with a woman, he could not banish it from his mind, and the fear of the same catastrophe befalling him grew so overwhelming that it prevented his own penis from stiffening. From then on, however much he desired a woman, he could not attain an erection, and the ignoble memory of every misadventure taunted and tyrannized him with increasing force.

Montaigne's friend had grown impotent after failing to achieve the unwavering rational command over his penis that he assumed to be an indispensable feature of normal manhood. Montaigne did not blame the penis: 'Except for genuine impotence, never again are you incapable if you are capable of doing it once.' It was the oppressive notion that we had complete mental control over our bodies, and the horror of departing from this portrait of normality, that had left the man unable to perform. The solution was to redraw the portrait; it was by accepting a loss of command over the penis as a harmless possibility in love-making that one could pre-empt its occurrence – as the stricken man eventually discovered. In bed with a woman, he learnt to:

> admit beforehand that he was subject to this infirmity and spoke openly about it, so relieving the tensions within his soul. By bearing the malady as something to be expected, his sense of constriction grew less and weighed less heavily on him.

Montaigne's frankness allowed the tensions in the reader's own soul to be relieved. The penis's abrupt moods were removed from the Cimmerian recesses of wordless shame and reconsidered with the unshockable, worldly eye of a philosopher whom nothing bodily could repulse. A sense of personal culpability was lessened by what Montaigne described as:

> [The universal] disobedience of this member which thrusts itself forward so inopportunely when we do not want it to, and which so inopportunely lets us down when we most need it.

A man who failed with his mistress and was unable to do any more than mumble an apology could regain his forces and soothe the anxieties of his beloved by accepting that his impotence belonged to a broad realm of sexual mishaps, neither very rare nor very peculiar. Montaigne knew a Gascon nobleman who, after failing to maintain an erection with a woman, fled home, cut off his penis and sent it to the lady 'to atone for his offence'. Montaigne proposed instead that:

> If [couples] are not ready, they should not try to rush things. Rather than fall into perpetual wretchedness by being struck with despair at a first rejection, it is better . . . to wait for an opportune moment . . . a man who suffers a rejection should make gentle assays and overtures with various little sallies; he should not stubbornly persist in proving himself inadequate once and for all.

It was a new language, unsensational and intimate, with which to articulate the loneliest moments of our sexuality. Cutting a path into the private sorrows of the bedchamber, Montaigne drained them of their ignominy, attempting all the while to reconcile us to our bodily selves. His courage in mentioning what is secretly lived but rarely heard expands the range of what we can dare to express to our lovers and to ourselves – a courage founded on Montaigne's conviction that nothing that can happen to man is inhuman, that 'every man bears the whole Form of the human condition,' a condition which includes – we do not need to blush nor hate ourselves for it – the risk of an occasional rebellious flaccidity in the penis.

Montaigne attributed our problems with our bodies in part to an absence of honest discussion about them in polite circles.

Representative stories and images do not tend to identify feminine grace with a strong interest in love-making, nor authority with the possession of a sphincter or penis. Pictures of kings and ladies do not encourage us to think of these eminent souls breaking wind or making love. Montaigne filled out the picture in blunt, beautiful French:

> *Au plus eslevé throne du monde si ne sommes assis que sus nostre cul.*
>
> Upon the highest throne in the world, we are seated, still, upon our arses.
>
> *Les Roys et les philosophes fientent, et les dames aussi.*
>
> Kings and philosophers shit: and so do ladies.

King Henri III   Catherine de' Medici

He could have put it otherwise. Instead of *'cul'*, *'derrière'* or *'fesses'*. Instead of *'fienter'*, *'aller au cabinet'*. Randle Cotgrave's *Dictionarie of the French and English Tongues* (*for the furtherance of young Learners, and the advantage of all others that endeavour to arrive at the most exactly knowledge of the French language*), printed in London in 1611, explained that *'fienter'* referred particularly to the excretions of vermin and badgers. If Montaigne felt the need for such strong language, it was to correct an equally strong denial of the body in works of philosophy and in drawing rooms. The view that ladies never had to wash their hands and kings had no behinds had made it timely to remind the world that they shat and had arses:

> The genital activities of mankind are so natural, so necessary and so right: what have they done to make us never dare to mention them without embarrassment and to exclude them from serious orderly conversation? We are not afraid to utter the words *kill*, *thieve*, or *betray*; but those others we only dare to mutter through our teeth.

In the vicinity of Montaigne's château were several beech-tree forests, one to the north near the village of Castillon-la-Bataille, another to the east near St Vivien. Montaigne's daughter Léonor must have known their silences and their grandeur. She was not encouraged to know their name: the French for 'beech tree' is *'fouteau'*. The French for 'fuck' is *'foutre'*.

'My daughter – I have no other children – is of an age when the more passionate girls are legally allowed to marry,' Montaigne explained of Léonor, then about fourteen:

> She is slender and gentle; by complexion she is young for her age, having been quietly brought up on her own by her mother; she is only just learning to throw off her childish innocence. She was reading from a French book in my presence when she came across the name of that well-known tree *fouteau*. The woman she has for governess pulled her up short rather rudely and made her jump over that awkward ditch.

Twenty coarse lackeys could not, Montaigne wryly remarked, have taught Léonor more about what lurked beneath *'fouteau'* than a stern injunction to longjump over the word. But for the governess, or the 'old crone' as her employer more bluntly termed her, the leap was essential because a young woman could not easily combine dignity with a knowledge of what might occur if in a few years' time she found herself in a bedroom with a man.

Montaigne was faulting our conventional portraits for leaving out so much of what we are. It was in part in order to correct this that he wrote his own book. When he retired at the age of thirty-eight, he wished to write, but was unsure what his theme should be. Only gradually did an idea form in his mind for a book so unusual as to be unlike any of the thousand volumes on the semicircular shelves.

He abandoned millennia of authorial coyness to write about himself. He set out to describe as explicitly as possible the workings of his own mind and body – declaring his intention in the preface to the *Essays*, two volumes of which were published in Bordeaux in 1580, with a third added in a Paris edition eight years later:

> Had I found myself among those peoples who are said still to live under the sweet liberty of Nature's primal laws, I can assure you that I would most willingly have portrayed myself whole, and wholly naked.

No author had hitherto aspired to present himself to his readers without any clothes on. There was no shortage of official, fully clothed portraits, accounts of the lives of saints and popes, Roman emperors and Greek statesmen. There was even an official portrait of Montaigne by Thomas de Leu (1562–*c*. 1620), which showed him dressed in the mayoral robes of the city, with the chain of the order of Saint-Michel offered to him by Charles IX in 1571, wearing an inscrutable, somewhat severe expression.

But this robed, Ciceronian self was not what Montaigne wished his *Essays* to reveal. He was concerned with the whole man, with the creation of an alternative to the portraits which had left out most of what man was. It was why his book came to include discussions of his meals, his penis, his stools, his sexual conquests and his farts – details which had seldom featured in a serious book before, so gravely did they flout man's image of himself as a rational creature. Montaigne informed his readers:

That the behaviour of his penis constituted an essential part of his identity:
Every one of my members, each as much as another, makes me myself: and none makes me more properly a man than that one. I owe to the public my portrait complete.

That he found sex noisy and messy:
Everywhere else you can preserve some decency; all other activities accept the rules of propriety: this other one can only be thought of as flawed or ridiculous. Just try and find a wise and discreet way of doing it!

That he liked quiet when sitting on the toilet:
Of all the natural operations, that is the one during which I least willingly tolerate being disrupted.

And that he was very regular about going:
My bowels and I never fail to keep our rendezvous, which is (unless some urgent business or illness disturbs us) when I jump out of bed.

If we accord importance to the kind of portraits which surround us, it is because we fashion our lives according to their example, accepting aspects of ourselves if they concur with what others mention of themselves. What we see evidence for in others, we will attend to within, what others are silent about, we may stay blind to or experience only in shame.

When I picture to myself the most reflective and the most wise of men in [sexual] postures, I hold it as an effrontery that he should claim to be reflective and wise.

It is not that wisdom is impossible, rather it is the definition of wisdom that Montaigne was seeking to nuance. True wisdom must involve an accommodation with our baser selves, it must adopt a modest view about the role that intelligence and high culture can play in any life and accept the urgent and at times deeply un-edifying demands of our mortal frame. Epicurean and Stoic philosophies had suggested that we could achieve mastery over our bodies, and never be swept away by our physical and passion-ate selves. It is noble advice that taps into our highest aspirations. It is also impossible, and therefore counter-productive:

> What is the use of those high philosophical peaks on which no human being can settle and those rules which exceed our practice and our power?

> It is not very clever of [man] to tailor his obligations to the standards of a different kind of being.

The body cannot be denied nor overcome, but there is at least, as Montaigne wished to remind the 'old crone', no need to choose between our dignity and an interest in *fouteau*:

> May we not say that there is nothing in us during this earthly prison either purely corporeal or purely spiritual and that it is injurious to tear a living man apart?

3
On Cultural Inadequacy

Another cause of a sense of inadequacy is the speed and arrogance with which people seem to divide the world into two camps, the camp of the *normal* and that of the *abnormal*. Our experiences and beliefs are liable frequently to be dismissed with a quizzical, slightly alarmed, 'Really? How weird!', accompanied by a raised eyebrow, amounting in a small way to a denial of our legitimacy and humanity.

In the summer of 1580, Montaigne acted on the desire of a lifetime, and made his first journey outside France, setting off on horseback to Rome via Germany, Austria and Switzerland. He travelled in the company of four young noblemen, including his brother, Bertrand de Mattecoulon, and a dozen servants. They were to be away from home for seventeen months, covering 3,000 miles. Among other towns, the party rode through Basle, Baden, Schaffhausen, Augsburg, Innsbruck, Verona, Venice, Padua, Bologna, Florence and Siena – finally reaching Rome towards evening on the last day of November 1580.

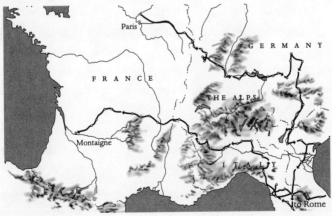

As the party travelled, Montaigne observed how people's ideas of what was normal altered sharply from province to province. In inns in the Swiss cantons, they thought it normal that beds should be raised high off the ground, so that one needed steps to climb into them, that there should be pretty curtains around them and that travellers should have rooms to themselves. A few miles away, in Germany, it was thought normal that beds should be low on the ground, have no curtains around them and that travellers should sleep four to a room. Innkeepers there offered feather quilts rather than the sheets one found in French inns. In Basle, people didn't mix water with their wine and had six or seven courses for dinner, and in Baden they ate only fish on Wednesdays. The smallest Swiss village was guarded by at least two policemen; the Germans rang their bells every quarter of an hour, in certain towns, every minute. In Lindau, they served soup made of quinces, the meat dish came before the soup, and the bread was made with fennel.

French travellers were prone to be very upset by the differences. In hotels, they kept away from sideboards with strange foods, requesting the normal dishes they knew from home. They tried not to talk to anyone who had made the error of not speaking their language, and picked gingerly at the fennel bread. Montaigne watched them from his table:

> Once out of their villages, they feel like fish out of water. Wherever they go they cling to their ways and curse foreign ones. If they come across a fellow-countryman ... they celebrate the event ... With a morose and taciturn prudence they travel about wrapped up in their cloaks and protecting themselves from the contagion of an unknown clime.

In the middle of the fifteenth century, in the southern German states, a new method of heating homes had been developed: the *Kastenofen*, a freestanding box-shaped iron stove made up of rectangular plates bolted together, in which coal or wood could be burnt. In the long winters, the advantages were great. Closed stoves could dispense four times the heat of an open fire, yet demanded less fuel and no chimney-sweeps. The heat was absorbed by the casing and spread slowly and evenly through the air. Poles were fixed around the stoves for airing and drying laundry, and families could use their stoves as seating areas throughout the winter.

But the French were not impressed. They found open fires cheaper to build; they accused German stoves of not providing a source of light and of withdrawing too much moisture from the air, lending an oppressive feeling to a room.

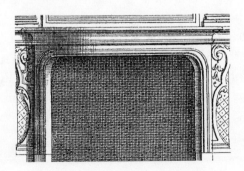

The subject was a matter of regional incomprehension. In Augsburg in October 1580, Montaigne met a German who delivered a lengthy critique of the way French people heated their houses with open fires, and who then went on to adumbrate the advantages of the iron stove. On hearing that Montaigne would be spending only a few days in the town (he had arrived on the 15th and was to leave on the 19th), he expressed pity for him, citing among the chief inconveniences of leaving Augsburg the 'heavy-headedness' he would suffer on returning to open fires – the very same 'heavy-headedness' which the French had long condemned iron stoves for provoking.

Montaigne examined the issue at close quarters. In Baden, he was assigned a room with an iron stove, and once he had grown used to a certain smell it released, spent a comfortable night. He noted that the stove enabled him to dress without putting on a furred gown, and months later, on a cold night in Italy, expressed regret at the absence of stoves in his inn.

On his return home, he weighed up the respective qualities of each heating system:

> It is true that the stoves give out an oppressive heat and that the materials of which they are built produce a smell when hot which causes headaches in those who are not used to them ... On the other hand, since the heat they give out is even, constant and spread all-over, without the visible flame, smoke and the draught produced by our chimneys, it has plenty of grounds for standing comparison with ours.

So what annoyed Montaigne were the firm, unexamined convictions of both the Augsburg gentleman and the French that their own system of heating was superior. Had Montaigne returned from Germany and installed in his library an iron stove from Augsburg, his countrymen would have greeted the object with the suspicion they accorded anything new:

Each nation has many customs and practices which are not only unknown to another nation but barbarous and a cause of wonder.

When there was of course nothing barbarous nor wondrous about either a stove or a fireplace. The definition of normality proposed by any given society seems to capture only a fraction of what is in fact reasonable, unfairly condemning vast areas of experience to an alien status. By pointing out to the man from Augsburg and his Gascon neighbours that an iron stove and an open fireplace had a legitimate place in the vast realm of acceptable heating systems, Montaigne was attempting to broaden his readers' provincial conception of the normal – and following in the footsteps of his favourite philosopher:

When they asked Socrates where he came from, he did not say 'From Athens', but 'From the world.'

This world had recently revealed itself to be far more peculiar than anyone in Europe had ever expected. On Friday 12 October 1492, forty-one years before Montaigne's birth, Christopher Columbus reached one of the islands on the archipelago of the Bahamas at the entrance of the gulf of Florida, and made contact with some Guanahani Indians, who had never heard of Jesus and walked about without any clothes on.

Montaigne took an avid interest. In the round library were several books on the life of the Indian tribes of America, among them Francisco Lopez de Gomara's *L'histoire générale des Indes*, Girolamo Benzoni's *Historia de mondo novo* and Jean de Léry's *Le voyage au Brésil*. He read that in South America, people liked to eat spiders, grasshoppers, ants, lizards and bats: 'They cook them and serve them up in various sauces.' There were American tribes in which virgins openly displayed their private parts, brides had orgies on their wedding day, men were allowed to marry each other, and the dead were boiled, pounded into a gruel, mixed with wine and drunk by their relatives at spirited parties. There were countries in which women stood up to pee and men squatted down, in which men let their hair grow on the front of their body, but shaved their back. There were countries in which men were circumcised, while in others, they had a horror of the tip of the penis ever seeing the light of day and so 'scrupulously stretched the foreskin right over it and tied it together with little cords'. There were nations in which you greeted people by turning your back to them, in which when the king spat, the court favourite held out a hand, and when he discharged his bowels, attendants 'gathered up his faeces in a linen cloth'. Every country seemed to have a different conception of beauty:

> In Peru, big ears are beautiful: they stretch them as far as they can, artificially. A man still alive today says that he saw in the East a country where this custom of stretching ears and loading them with jewels is held in such esteem that he was often able to thrust his arm, clothes and all, through the holes women pierced in their lobes. Elsewhere there are whole nations which carefully blacken their teeth and loathe seeing white ones. Elsewhere they dye them red ... The women of Mexico count low foreheads as a sign of beauty: so, while they pluck the hair from the rest of their body, there they encourage it to grow thick and propagate it artificially. They hold large breasts in such high esteem that they affect giving suck to their children over their shoulders.

From Jean de Léry, Montaigne learned that the Tupi tribes of Brazil walked around in Edenic nudity, and showed no trace of shame (indeed, when Europeans tried to offer the Tupi women clothes, they giggled and turned them down, puzzled why anyone would burden themselves with anything so uncomfortable).

Tant les hommes que la femme étaient aussi entièrement nus que quand ils sortirent du ventre de leur mère. Jean de Léry, *Voyage au Brésil* (1578)

De Léry's engraver (who had spent eight years with the tribes) took care to correct the rumour rife in Europe that the Tupis were as hairy as animals (de Léry: '*Ils ne sont point naturellement poilus que nous ne sommes en ce pays*'). The men shaved their heads, and the women grew their hair long, and tied it together with pretty red braids. The Tupi Indians loved to wash; any time they saw a river, they would jump into it and rub each other down. They might wash as many as twelve times a day.

They lived in long barn-like structures which slept 200 people. Their beds were woven from cotton and slung between pillars like hammocks (when they went hunting, the Tupis took their beds with them, and had afternoon naps suspended between trees). Every six months, a village would move to a new location, because the inhabitants felt a change of scene would do them good ('*Ils n'ont d'autre réponse, sinon de dire que changeant l'air, ils se portent mieux'* – de Léry). The Tupis' existence was so well ordered, they frequently lived to be a hundred and never had white or grey hair in old age. They were also extremely hospitable. When a newcomer arrived in a village, the women would cover their faces, start crying, and exclaim, 'How are you? You've taken such trouble to come and visit us!' Visitors would immediately be offered the favourite Tupi drink, made from the root of a plant and coloured like claret, which tasted sharp but was good for the stomach.

Tupi men were allowed to take more than one wife, and were said to be devoted to them all. 'Their entire system of ethics contains only the same two articles: resoluteness in battle and love of their wives,' reported Montaigne. And the wives were apparently happy with the arrangement, showing no jealousy (sexual relations were relaxed, the only prohibition being that one should never sleep with close relatives). Montaigne, with his wife downstairs in the castle, relished the detail:

> One beautiful characteristic of their marriages is worth noting: just as our wives are zealous in thwarting our love and tenderness for other women, theirs are equally zealous in obtaining them for them. Being more concerned for their husband's reputation than for anything else, they take care and trouble to have as many fellow-wives as possible, since that is a testimony to their husband's valour.

It was all undeniably peculiar. Montaigne did not find any of it abnormal.

He was in a minority. Soon after Columbus's discovery, Spanish and Portuguese colonists arrived from Europe to exploit the new lands and decided that the natives were little better than animals. The Catholic knight Villegagnon spoke of them as 'beasts with a human face' (*'ce sont des bêtes portant figure humaine'*); the Calvinist minister Richer argued they had no moral sense (*'l'hébétude crasse de leur esprit ne distingue pas le bien du mal'*); and the doctor Laurent Joubert, after examining five Brazilian women, asserted that they had no periods and therefore categorically did not belong to the human race.

Having stripped them of their humanity, the Spanish began to slaughter them like animals. By 1534, forty-two years after Columbus's arrival, the Aztec and Inca empires had been destroyed, and their peoples enslaved or murdered. Montaigne read of the barbarism in Bartolomeo Las Casas's *Brevissima Relación de la Destrucción de las Indias* (printed in Seville in 1552, translated into French in 1580 by Jacques de Miggrode as *Tyrannies et cruautés des Espagnols perpétrées es Indes occidentales qu'on dit le Nouveau Monde*). The Indians were undermined by their own hospitality and by the weakness of their arms. They opened their villages and cities to the Spanish, to find their guests turning on them when they were least prepared. Their primitive weapons were no match for Spanish cannons and swords, and the *conquistadores* showed no mercy towards their victims. They killed children, slit open the bellies of pregnant women, gouged out eyes, roasted whole families alive and set fire to villages in the night.

They trained dogs to go into the jungles where the Indians had fled and to tear them to pieces.

Men were sent to work in gold- and silver-mines, chained together by iron collars. When a man died, his body was cut from the chain, while his companions on either side continued working. Most Indians did not last more than three weeks in the mines. Women were raped and disfigured in front of their husbands.

The favoured form of mutilation was to slice chins and noses. Las Casas told how one woman, seeing the Spanish armies advancing with their dogs, hanged herself with her child. A soldier arrived, cut the child in two with his sword, gave one half to his dogs, then asked a friar to administer last rites so that the infant would be assured a place in Christ's heaven.

With men and women separated from each other, desolate and anxious, the Indians committed suicide in large numbers. Between Montaigne's birth in 1533 and the publication of the third book of his *Essays* in 1588, the native population of the New World is estimated to have dropped from 80 to 10 million inhabitants.

The Spanish had butchered the Indians with a clean conscience because they were confident that they knew what a normal human being was. Their reason told them it was someone who wore breeches, had one wife, didn't eat spiders and slept in a bed:

> We could understand nothing of their language; their manners and even their features and clothing were far different from ours. Which of us did not take them for brutes and savages? Which of us

did not attribute their silence to dullness and brutish ignorance? After all, they . . . were unaware of our hand-kissings and our low and complex bows.

They might have seemed like human beings: 'Ah! But they wear no breeches . . .'

Behind the butchery lay messy reasoning. Separating the normal from the abnormal typically proceeds through a form of inductive logic, whereby we infer a general law from particular instances (as logicians would put it, from observing that A1 is ø, A2 is ø and A3 is ø, we come to the view that 'All As are ø'). Seeking to judge whether someone is intelligent, we look for features common to everyone intelligent we have met hitherto. If we met an intelligent person who looked like 1, another who looked like 2, and a third like 3, we are likely to decide that intelligent people read a lot, dress in black and look rather solemn. There is a danger we will dismiss as stupid, and perhaps later kill, someone who looks like 4.

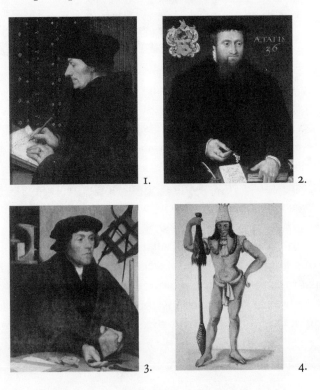

1.   2.

3.   4.

French travellers who reacted in horror to German stoves in their bedrooms would have known a number of good fireplaces in their country before arriving in Germany. One would perhaps have looked like 1, another like 2, a third like 3, and from this they would have concluded that the essence of a good heating system was an open hearth.

1.

2.

3.

Montaigne bemoaned the intellectual arrogance at play. There *were* savages in South America; they were not the ones eating spiders:

> Every man calls barbarous anything he is not accustomed to; we have no other criterion of truth or right-reason than the example and form of the opinions and customs of our own country. There we always find the perfect religion, the perfect polity, the most developed and perfect way of doing anything!

He was not attempting to do away with the distinction between barbarous and civilized; there were differences in value between the customs of countries (cultural relativism being as crude as nationalism). He was correcting the way we made the distinction. Our country might have many virtues, but these did not depend on it being *our* country. A foreign land might have many faults, but these could not be identified through the mere fact that its customs were unusual. Nationality and familiarity were absurd criteria by which to decide on the good.

French custom had decreed that if one had an impediment in the nasal passage, one should blow it into a handkerchief. But Montaigne had a friend who, having reflected on the matter, had come to the view that it might be better to blow one's nose straight into one's fingers:

> Defending his action . . . he asked me why that filthy mucus should
> be so privileged that we should prepare fine linen to receive it and
> then should wrap it up and carry it carefully about on our persons
> . . . I considered that what he said was not totally unreasonable, but
> habit had prevented me from noticing just that strangeness which
> we find so hideous in similar customs in another country.

Careful reasoning rather than prejudice was to be the means of evaluating behaviour, Montaigne's frustration caused by those who blithely equated the unfamiliar with the inadequate and so ignored the most basic lesson in intellectual humility offered by the greatest of the ancient philosophers:

> The wisest man that ever was, when asked what he knew, replied
> that the one thing he did know was that he knew nothing.

∽

What, then, should we do if we find ourselves facing a veiled suggestion of abnormality manifested in a quizzical, slightly alarmed 'Really? How weird!', accompanied by a raised eyebrow, amounting in its own small way to a denial of legitimacy and humanity – a reaction which Montaigne's friend had encountered in Gascony when he blew his nose into his fingers, and which had, in its most extreme form, led to the devastation of the South American tribes?

Perhaps we should remember the degree to which accusations of abnormality are regionally and historically founded. To loosen their hold on us, we need only expose ourselves to the diversity of customs across time and space. What is considered abnormal in one group at one moment may not, and will not always be deemed so. We may cross borders in our minds.

WHAT IS CONSIDERED ABNORMAL WHERE

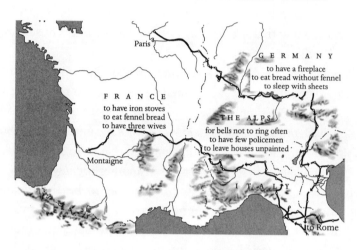

Montaigne had filled his library with books that helped him cross the borders of prejudice. There were history books, travel journals, the reports of missionaries and sea captains, the literatures of other lands and illustrated volumes with pictures of strangely clad tribes eating fish of unknown names. Through these books, Montaigne could gain legitimacy for parts of himself of which there was no evidence in the vicinity – the Roman parts, the Greek parts, the sides of himself that were more Mexican and Tupi than Gascon, the parts that would have liked to have six wives or have a shaved back or wash twelve times a day; he could feel less alone with these by turning to copies of Tacitus's *Annals*, Gonçalez de Mendoza's history of China, Goulart's history of Portugal, Lebelski's history of Persia, Leo Africanus's travels around Africa, Lusignano's history of Cyprus, Postel's collection of Turkish and oriental histories and Muenster's universal cosmography (which promised pictures of 'animaulx estranges').

If he felt oppressed by the claims made by others to universal truth, he could in a similar way line up the theories of the universe held by all the great ancient philosophers and then witness, despite the confidence of each thinker that he was in possession of the whole truth, the ludicrous divergence that resulted. After such comparative study, Montaigne sarcastically confessed to having no clue whether to accept:

> the 'Ideas' of Plato, the atoms of Epicurus, the plenum and vacuum of Leucippus and Democritus, the water of Thales, the infinity of Nature of Anaximander, or the aether of Diogenes, the numbers and symmetry of Pythagoras, the infinity of Parmenides, the Unity of Musaeus, the fire and water of Apollodorus, the homogeneous particles of Anaxagoras, the discord and concord of Empedocles, the fire of Heraclitus, or any other opinion drawn from the boundless confusion of judgement and doctrines produced by our fine human reason, with all its certainty and perspicuity.

The discoveries of new worlds and ancient texts powerfully undermined what Montaigne described as 'that distressing and combative arrogance which has complete faith and trust in itself':

> Anyone who made an intelligent collection of the asinine stupidities of human wisdom would have a wondrous tale to tell . . . We can judge what we should think of Man, of his sense and of his reason, when we find such obvious and gross errors even in these important characters who have raised human intelligence to great heights.

It also helped to have spent seventeen months journeying around Europe on horseback. Testimony of other countries and ways of life alleviated the oppressive atmosphere of Montaigne's own region. What one society judged to be strange, another might more sensibly welcome as normal.

Other lands may return to us a sense of possibility stamped out by provincial arrogance; they encourage us to grow more acceptable to ourselves. The conception of the normal proposed by any particular province – Athens, Augsburg, Cuzco, Mexico, Rome, Seville, Gascony – has room for only a few aspects of our nature, and unfairly consigns the rest to the barbaric and bizarre. Every man may bear the whole form of the human condition, but it seems that no single country can tolerate the complexity of this condition.

Among the fifty-seven inscriptions that Montaigne had painted on the beams of his library ceiling, was a line from Terence:

> *Homo sum, humani a me nihil alienum puto.*

I am a man, nothing human is foreign to me.

By travelling across frontiers, on horseback and in the imagination, Montaigne invited us to exchange local prejudices and the self-division they induced for less constraining identities as citizens of the world.

Another consolation for accusations of abnormality is friendship, a friend being, among other things, someone kind enough to consider more of us normal than most people do. We may share judgements with friends that would in ordinary company be censured for being too caustic, sexual, despairing, daft, clever or vulnerable – friendship a minor conspiracy against what other people think of as reasonable.

Like Epicurus, Montaigne believed friendship to be an essential component of happiness:

> In my judgement the sweetness of well-matched and compatible fellowship can never cost too dear. O! a friend! How true is that ancient judgement, that the frequenting of one is more sweet than the element water, more necessary than the element fire.

For a time, he was fortunate enough to know such fellowship. At the age of twenty-five, he was introduced to a twenty-eight-year-old writer and member of the Bordeaux Parlement, Étienne de La Boétie. It was friendship at first sight:

> We were seeking each other before we set eyes on each other because of the reports we had heard . . . we embraced each other by our names. And at our first meeting, which chanced to be at a great crowded town-festival, we found ourselves so taken with each other, so well acquainted, so bound together, that from that time on nothing was so close to us as each other.

The friendship was of a kind, Montaigne believed, that only occurred once every 300 years; it had nothing in common with the tepid alliances frequently denoted by the term:

> What we normally call friends and friendships are no more than acquaintances and familiar relationships bound by some chance or some suitability, by means of which our souls support each other. In the friendship which I am talking about, souls are mingled and confounded in so universal a blending that they efface the seam which joins them together so that it cannot be found.

The friendship would not have been so valuable if most people had not been so disappointing – if Montaigne had not had to hide so much of himself from them. The depth of his attachment to La Boétie signalled the extent to which, in his interactions with others, he had been forced to present only an edited image of himself to avoid suspicion and raised eyebrows. Many years later, Montaigne analysed the source of his affections for La Boétie:

> *Luy seul jouyssoit de ma vraye image.*
>
> He alone had the privilege of my true portrait.

That is, La Boétie – uniquely among Montaigne's acquaintances – understood him properly. He allowed him to be himself; through his psychological acuity, he enabled him to be so. He offered scope for valuable and yet until then neglected dimensions of Montaigne's character – which suggests that we pick our friends not only because they are kind and enjoyable company, but also, perhaps more importantly, because they understand us for who we think we are.

The idyll was painfully brief. Four years after the first meeting, in August 1563, La Boétie fell ill with stomach cramps and died a few days later. The loss was to haunt Montaigne for ever:

> In truth if I compare the rest of my life . . . to those four years which I was granted to enjoy the sweet companionship and fellowship of a man like that, it is but smoke and ashes, a night dark and dreary. Since that day when I lost him . . . I merely drag wearily on.

Throughout the *Essays*, there were expressions of longing for a soul mate comparable to the dead companion. Eighteen years after La Boétie's death, Montaigne was still visited by periods of grief. In May 1581, in La Villa near Lucca, where he had gone to take the waters, he wrote in his travel journal that he had spent an entire day beset by 'painful thoughts about Monsieur de La Boétie. I was in this mood so long, without recovering, that it did me much harm.'

He was never to be blessed again in his friendships, but he discovered the finest form of compensation. In the *Essays*, he recreated in another medium the true portrait of himself that La Boétie had recognized. He became himself on the page as he had been himself in the company of his friend.

Authorship was prompted by disappointment with those in the vicinity, and yet it was infused with the hope that someone elsewhere would understand; his book an address to everyone and no one in particular. He was aware of the paradox of expressing his deepest self to strangers in bookshops:

> Many things that I would not care to tell any individual man I tell to the public, and for knowledge of my most secret thoughts, I refer my most loyal friends to a bookseller's stall.

And yet we should be grateful for the paradox. Booksellers are the most valuable destination for the lonely, given the numbers of books that were written because authors couldn't find anyone to talk to.

Montaigne might have begun writing to alleviate a personal sense of loneliness, but his book may serve in a small way to alleviate our own. One man's honest, unguarded portrait of himself – in which he mentions impotence and farting, in which he writes of his dead friend and explains that he needs quiet when sitting on the toilet – enables us to feel less singular about sides of ourselves that have gone unmentioned in normal company and normal portraits, but which, it seems, are no less a part of our reality.

4
On Intellectual Inadequacy

There are some leading assumptions about what it takes to be a clever person:

What clever people should know

One of them, reflected in what is taught in many schools and universities, is that clever people should know how to answer questions like:

1. Find the lengths or angles marked *x* in the following triangles.

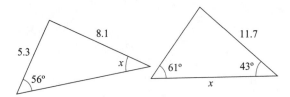

2. What are the subject term, predicate term, copula and quantifiers (if any) in the following sentences: Dogs are man's best friend; Lucilius is wicked; All bats are members of the class of rodents; Nothing green is in the room?

3. What is Thomas Aquinas's First Cause argument?

4. Translate:

Πᾶσα τέχνη καὶ πᾶσα μέθοδος, ὁμοίως δὲ πρᾶξίς τε καὶ
προαίρεσις, ἀγαθοῦ τινὸς ἐφίεσθαι δοκεῖ· διὸ καλῶς
ἀπεφήναντο τἀγαθὸν οὗ πάντ' ἐφίεται. (διαφορὰ δέ τις
φαίνεται τῶν τελῶν· τὰ μὲν γάρ εἰσιν ἐνέργειαι, τὰ δὲ παρ'
αὐτὰς ἔργα τινά· ὧν δ' εἰσὶ τέλη τινὰ παρὰ τὰς πράξεις, ἐν
τούτοις βελτίω πέφυκε τῶν ἐνεργειῶν τὰ ἔργα.) πολλῶν δὲ
πράξεών οὐσῶν καὶ τεχνῶν καὶ ἐπιστημῶν πολλὰ γίνεται
καὶ τὰ τέλη· ἰατρικῆς μὲν γὰρ ὑγίεια, ναυπηγικῆς δὲ πλοῖον,
στρατηγικῆς δὲ νίκη, οἰκονομικῆς δὲ πλοῦτος.

(Aristotle, *Nicomachean Ethics*, I i–iv)

5. Translate:

> *In capitis mei levitatem iocatus est et in oculorum valitudinem et*
> *in crurum gracilitatem et in staturam. Quae contumelia est quod*
> *apparet audire? Coram uno aliquid dictum ridemus, coram pluribus*
> *indignamur, et eorum aliis libertatem non relinquimus, quae ipsi*
> *in nos dicere adsuevimus; iocis temperatis delectamur, immodicis*
> *irascimur.*

(Seneca, *De Constantia*, XVI. 4)

Montaigne had faced many such questions and answered them well.
He was sent to one of France's best educational establishments,
the Collège de Guyenne in Bordeaux, founded in 1533 to replace the
city's old and inadequate Collège des Arts. By the time Michel
started attending classes there at the age of six, the school had developed a national reputation as a centre of learning. The staff included
an enlightened principal, André de Gouvéa, a renowned Greek
scholar, Nicolas de Grouchy, an Aristotelian scholar, Guillaume
Guerente, and the Scottish poet George Buchanan.

If one tries to define the philosophy of education underpinning
the Collège de Guyenne, or indeed that of most schools and universities before and after it, one might loosely suggest it to be based
on the idea that the more a student learns about the world (history,

science, literature), the better. But Montaigne, after following the curriculum at the Collège dutifully until graduation, added an important proviso:

> If man were wise, he would gauge the true worth of anything by its usefulness and appropriateness to his life.

Only that which makes us feel better may be worth understanding.

Two great thinkers of antiquity were likely to have featured prominently in the curriculum at the Collège de Guyenne and been held up as exemplars of intelligence. Students would have been introduced to Aristotle's *Prior* and *Posterior Analytics*, in which the Greek philosopher pioneered logic, and stated that if A is predicated of every B, and B of every C, necessarily A is predicated of every C. Aristotle argued that if a proposition says or denies P of S, then S and P are its terms, with P being the predicate term and S the subject term, and added that all propositions are either universal or particular, affirming or denying P of every S or part of S. Then there was the Roman scholar Marcus Terentius Varro, who assembled a library for Julius Caesar and wrote six hundred books, including an encyclopedia on the liberal arts and twenty-five books on etymology and linguistics.

Montaigne was not unmoved. It is a feat to write a shelf of books on the origins of words and to discover universal affirmatives. And yet if we were to find that those who did so were no happier or were indeed a little more unhappy than those who had never heard of philosophical logic, we might wonder. Montaigne considered the lives of Aristotle and Varro, and raised a question:

> What good did their great erudition do for Varro and Aristotle? Did it free them from human ills? Did it relieve them of misfortunes such as befall a common porter? Could logic console them for the gout . . .?

To understand why the two men could have been both so erudite and so unhappy, Montaigne distinguished between two categories of knowledge: *learning* and *wisdom*. In the category of learning he placed, among other subjects, logic, etymology, grammar, Latin and Greek. And in the category of wisdom, he placed a far broader, more elusive and more valuable kind of knowledge, everything that could help a person to live well, by which Montaigne meant, help them to live happily and morally.

The problem with the Collège de Guyenne, despite its professional staff and principal, was that it excelled at imparting learning but failed entirely at imparting wisdom – repeating at an institutional level the errors that had marred the personal lives of Varro and Aristotle:

> I gladly come back to the theme of the absurdity of our education: its end has not been to make us good and wise, but learned. And it has succeeded. It has not taught us to seek virtue and to embrace wisdom: it has impressed upon us their derivation and their etymology . . .
>
> We readily inquire, 'Does he know Greek or Latin?' 'Can he write poetry and prose?' But what matters most is what we put last: 'Has he become better and wiser?' We ought to find out not who understands *most* but who understands *best*. We work merely to fill the memory, leaving the understanding and the sense of right and wrong empty.

He had never been good at sport: 'At dancing, tennis and wrestling I have not been able to acquire more than a slight, vulgar skill; and at swimming, fencing, vaulting and jumping, no skill at all.' Nevertheless, so strong was Montaigne's objection to the lack of wisdom imparted by most schoolteachers, that he did not shrink from suggesting a drastic alternative to the classroom for the youth of France.

If our souls do not move with a better motion and if we do not have a healthier judgement, then I would just as soon that a pupil spend his time playing tennis.

He would of course have preferred students to go to school, but schools that taught them wisdom rather than the etymology of the word and could correct the long-standing intellectual bias towards abstract questions. Thales from Miletus in Asia Minor was an early example of the bias, celebrated throughout the ages for having in the sixth century BC tried to measure the heavens and for having determined the height of the Great Pyramid of Egypt according to the theorem of similar triangles – a complicated and dazzling achievement, no doubt, but not what Montaigne wished to see dominate his curriculum. He had greater sympathy with the implicit educational philosophy of one of Thales's impudent young acquaintances:

> I have always felt grateful to that girl from Miletus who, seeing the local philosopher ... with his eyes staring upwards, constantly occupied in contemplating the vault of heaven, tripped him up, to warn him that there was time enough to occupy his thoughts with things above the clouds when he had accounted for everything lying before his feet ... You can make exactly the same reproach as that woman made against Thales against anyone concerned with philosophy: he fails to see what lies before his feet.

Montaigne noted in other areas a similar tendency to privilege extraordinary activities over humbler but no less important ones – and just like the girl from Miletus, tried to bring us back to earth:

> Storming a breach, conducting an embassy, ruling a nation are glittering deeds. Rebuking, laughing, buying, selling, loving, hating and living together gently and justly with your household – and with yourself – not getting slack nor being false to yourself, is something more remarkable, more rare and more difficult. Whatever people may say, such secluded lives sustain in that way duties which are at least as hard and as tense as those of other lives.

So what would Montaigne have wished pupils to learn at school? What kind of examinations could have tested for the wise intelligence he had in mind, one so far removed from the mental skills of the unhappy Aristotle and Varro?

The examinations would have raised questions about the challenges of quotidian life: love, sex, illness, death, children, money and ambition.

An examination in Montaignean wisdom

1. About seven or eight years ago, some two leagues from here, there was a villager, who is still alive; his brain had long been battered by his wife's jealousy; one day he came home from work to be welcomed by her usual nagging; it made him so mad that, taking the sickle he still had in his hand he suddenly lopped off the members which put her into such a fever and chucked them in her face. (*Essays*, II.29)
    a) How should one settle domestic disputes?
    b) Was the wife nagging or expressing affection?

2. Consider these two quotations:
    I want death to find me planting my cabbages, neither worrying about it nor the unfinished gardening. (*Essays*, I.20)
    I can scarcely tell my cabbages from my lettuces. (*Essays*, II.17)
    What is a wise approach to death?

3. It is perhaps a more chaste and fruitful practice to bring women
    to learn early what the living reality [of penis size] is rather than
    to allow them to make conjectures according to the licence of a
    heated imagination: instead of our organs as they are, their hopes
    and desires lead them to substitute extravagant ones three times
    as big . . . What great harm is done by those graffiti of enormous
    genitals which boys scatter over the corridors and staircases of
    our royal palaces! From them arises a cruel misunderstanding of
    our natural capacities. (*Essays*, III.5)

    How should a man with a small 'living reality' bring up the
    subject?

4. I know of a squire who had entertained a goodly company in his
    hall and then, four or five days later, boasted as a joke (for there
    was no truth in it) that he had made them eat cat pie; one of the
    young ladies in the party was struck with such a horror at this
    that she collapsed with a serious stomach disorder and a fever: it
    was impossible to save her. (*Essays*, I.21)

    Analyse the distribution of moral responsibility.

5. If only talking to oneself did not look mad, no day would go by
    without my being heard growling to myself, against myself, 'You
    silly shit!' (*Essays*, I.38)

    The most uncouth of our afflictions is to despise our being.
    (*Essays*, III.13)

    How much love should one have for oneself?

Setting people examination papers measuring wisdom rather than
learning would probably result in an immediate realignment of the
hierarchy of intelligence – and a surprising new élite. Montaigne
delighted in the prospect of the incongruous people who would
now be recognized as cleverer than the lauded but often unworthy
traditional candidates.

I have seen in my time hundreds of craftsmen and ploughmen wiser and happier than university rectors.

What clever people should sound and look like

It is common to assume that we are dealing with a highly intelligent book when we cease to understand it. Profound ideas cannot, after all, be explained in the language of children. Yet the association between difficulty and profundity might less generously be described as a manifestation in the literary sphere of a perversity familiar from emotional life, where people who are mysterious and elusive can inspire a respect in modest minds that reliable and clear ones do not.

Montaigne had no qualms bluntly admitting his problem with mysterious books. 'I cannot have lengthy commerce with [them],' he wrote, 'I only like pleasurable, easy [ones] which tickle my interest.'

> I am not prepared to bash my brains for anything, not even for learning's sake, however precious it may be. From books all I seek is to give myself pleasure by an honourable pastime . . . If I come across difficult passages in my reading I never bite my nails over them: after making a charge or two I let them be . . . If one book wearies me I take up another.

Which was nonsense, or rather playful posturing on the part of a man with a thousand volumes on his shelf and an encyclopedic knowledge of Greek and Latin philosophy. If Montaigne enjoyed presenting himself as a dim gentleman prone to somnolence during philosophical expositions, it was disingenuousness with a purpose. The repeated declarations of laziness and slowness were tactical ways to undermine a corrupt understanding of intelligence and good writing.

There are, so Montaigne implied, no legitimate reasons why books in the humanities should be difficult or boring; wisdom does not require a specialized vocabulary or syntax, nor does an audience benefit from being wearied. Carefully used, boredom can be a valuable indicator of the merit of books. Though it can never be a sufficient judge (and in its more degenerate forms, slips into wilful indifference and impatience), taking our levels of boredom into account can temper an otherwise excessive tolerance for balderdash. Those who do not listen to their boredom when reading, like those who pay no attention to pain, may be increasing their suffering unnecessarily. Whatever the dangers of being wrongly bored, there are as many pitfalls in never allowing ourselves to lose patience with our reading matter.

Every difficult work presents us with a choice of whether to judge the author inept for not being clear, or ourselves stupid for not grasping what is going on. Montaigne encouraged us to blame the author. An incomprehensible prose-style is likely to have resulted more from laziness than cleverness; what reads easily is rarely so written. Or else such prose masks an absence of content; being incomprehensible offers unparalleled protection against having nothing to say:

> Difficulty is a coin which the learned conjure with so as not to reveal the vanity of their studies and which human stupidity is keen to accept in payment.

There is no reason for philosophers to use words that would sound out of place in a street or market:

> Just as in dress it is the sign of a petty mind to seek to draw attention by some personal or unusual fashion, so too in speech; the search for new expressions and little-known words derives from an adolescent schoolmasterish ambition. If only I could limit myself to words used in Les Halles in Paris.

But writing with simplicity requires courage, for there is a danger that one will be overlooked, dismissed as simpleminded by those with a tenacious belief that impassable prose is a hallmark of intelligence. So strong is this bias, Montaigne wondered whether the majority of university scholars would have appreciated Socrates, a man they professed to revere above all others, if he had approached them in their own towns, devoid of the prestige of Plato's dialogues, in his dirty cloak, speaking in plain language:

> The portrait of the conversations of Socrates which his friends have bequeathed to us receives our approbation only because we are overawed by the general approval of them. It is not from our own knowledge; since they do not follow our practices: if something like them were to be produced nowadays there are few who would rate them highly. We can appreciate no graces which are not pointed, inflated and magnified by artifice. Such graces as flow on under the name of naivety and simplicity readily go unseen by so coarse an insight as ours ... For us, is not naivety close kin to simplemindedness and a quality worthy of reproach? Socrates makes his soul move with the natural motion of the common people: thus speaks a peasant; thus speaks a woman ... His inductions and comparisons are drawn from the most ordinary and best-known of men's activities; anyone can understand him. Under so common a form we today would never have discerned the nobility and splendour of his astonishing concepts; we who judge any which are not swollen up by erudition to be base and commonplace and who are never aware of riches except when pompously paraded.

It is a plea to take books seriously, even when their language is unintimidating and their ideas clear – and, by extension, to refrain from considering ourselves as fools if, because of a hole in our budget or our education, our cloaks are simple and our vocabulary no larger than that of a stallholder in Les Halles.

What clever people should know

They should know the facts, and if they do not and if they have in addition been so foolish as to get these wrong in a book, they should expect no mercy from scholars, who will be justified in slapping them down, and pointing out, with supercilious civility, that a date is wrong or a word misquoted, a passage is out of context or an important source forgotten.

Yet in Montaigne's schema of intelligence, what matters in a book is usefulness and appropriateness to life; it is less valuable to convey with precision what Plato wrote or Epicurus meant than to judge whether what they have said is interesting and could in the early hours help us over anxiety or loneliness. The responsibility of authors in the humanities is not to quasi-scientific accuracy, but to happiness and health. Montaigne vented his irritation with those who refused the point:

> The scholars whose concern it is to pass judgement on books recognize no worth but that of learning and allow no intellectual activity other than that of scholarship and erudition. Mistake one Scipio for the other, and you have nothing left worth saying, have you! According to them, fail to know your Aristotle and you fail to know yourself.

The *Essays* were themselves marked by frequent misquotations, misattributions, illogical swerves of argument and a failure to define terms. The author wasn't bothered:

> I do my writing at home, deep in the country, where nobody can help or correct me and where I normally never frequent anybody

who knows even the Latin of the Lord's prayer let alone proper
French.
Naturally there were errors in the book ('I am full of them,' he
boasted), but they weren't enough to doom the *Essays*, just as accuracy could not ensure their worth. It was a greater sin to write
something which did not attempt to be wise than to confuse Scipio
Aemilianus (*c.* 185–129 BC) with Scipio Africanus (236–183 BC).

Where clever people should get their ideas from

From people even cleverer than they are. They should spend their
time quoting and producing commentaries about great authorities
who occupy the upper rungs of the tree of knowledge. They
should write treatises on the moral thought of Plato or the ethics of
Cicero.

Montaigne owed much to the idea. There were frequent passages
of commentary in the *Essays*, and hundreds of quotations from
authors who Montaigne felt had captured points more elegantly
and more acutely than he was able to. He quoted Plato 128 times,
Lucretius 149 and Seneca 130.

It is tempting to quote authors when they express our very own
thoughts but with a clarity and psychological accuracy we cannot
match. They know us better than we know ourselves. What is shy
and confused in us is succinctly and elegantly phrased in them, our
pencil lines and annotations in the margins of their books and our
borrowings from them indicating where we find a piece of ourselves, a sentence or two built of the very substance of which our
own minds are made – a congruence all the more striking if the
work was written in an age of togas and animal sacrifices. We
invite these words into our books as a homage for reminding us of
who we are.

But rather than illuminating our experiences and goading us on to our own discoveries, great books may come to cast a problematic shadow. They may lead us to dismiss aspects of our lives of which there is no printed testimony. Far from expanding our horizons, they may unjustly come to mark their limits. Montaigne knew one man who seemed to have bought his bibliophilia too dearly:

> Whenever I ask [this] acquaintance of mine to tell me what he knows about something, he wants to show me a book: he would not venture to tell me that he has scabs on his arse without studying his lexicon to find out the meanings of *scab* and *arse*.

Such reluctance to trust our own, extra-literary, experiences might not be grievous if books could be relied upon to express all our potentialities, if they knew all our scabs. But as Montaigne recognized, the great books are silent on too many themes, so that if we allow them to define the boundaries of our curiosity, they will hold back the development of our minds. A meeting in Italy crystallized the issue:

> In Pisa I met a decent man who is such an Aristotelian that the most basic of his doctrines is that the touchstone and the measuring-scale of all sound ideas and of each and every truth must lie in conformity with the teachings of Aristotle, outside of which all is inane and chimerical: Aristotle has seen everything, done everything.

He had, of course, done and seen a lot. Of all the thinkers of antiquity, Aristotle was perhaps the most comprehensive, his works ranging over the landscape of knowledge (*On Generation and Corruption, On the Heavens, Meteorology, On the Soul, Parts of Animals, Movements of Animals, Sophistical Refutations, Nicomachean Ethics, Physics, Politics*).

But the very scale of Aristotle's achievement bequeathed a problematic legacy. There are authors too clever for our own good. Having said so much, they appear to have had the last word. Their genius inhibits the sense of irreverence vital to creative work in their successors. Aristotle may, paradoxically, prevent those who most respect him from behaving like him. He rose to greatness only by doubting much of the knowledge that had been built up before him, not by refusing to read Plato or Heraclitus, but by mounting a salient critique of some of their weaknesses based on an appreciation of their strengths. To act in a truly Aristotelian spirit, as Montaigne realized and the man from Pisa did not, may mean allowing for some intelligent departures from even the most accomplished authorities.

Yet it is understandable to prefer to quote and write commentaries rather than speak and think for ourselves. A commentary on a book written by someone else, though technically laborious to produce, requiring hours of research and exegesis, is immune from the most cruel attacks that can befall original works. Commentators may be criticized for failing to do justice to the ideas of great thinkers; they cannot be held responsible for the ideas themselves – which was a reason why Montaigne included so many quotations and passages of commentary in the *Essays*:

> I sometimes get others to say what I cannot put so well myself because of the weakness of my language, and sometimes because of the weakness of my intellect ... *[and] sometimes ... to rein in the temerity of those hasty criticisms which leap to attack writings of every kind, especially recent writings by men still alive ... I have to hide my weaknesses beneath those great reputations.*

It is striking how much more seriously we are likely to be taken after we have been dead a few centuries. Statements which might be acceptable when they issue from the quills of ancient authors are likely to attract ridicule when expressed by contemporaries. Critics are not inclined to bow before the grander pronouncements of those with whom they attended university. It is not these individuals who will be allowed to speak *as though they were ancient philosophers*. 'No man has escaped paying the penalty for being born,' wrote Seneca, but a man struck by a similar sentiment in later ages would not be advised to speak like this unless he manifested a particular appetite for humiliation. Montaigne, who did not, took shelter, and at the end of the *Essays*, made a confession, touching for its vulnerability:

> If I had had confidence to do what I really wanted, I would have spoken utterly alone, come what may.

If he lacked confidence, it was because the closer one came to him in time and place, the less his thoughts were likely to be treated as though they might be as valid as those of Seneca and Plato:

> In my own climate of Gascony, they find it funny to see me in print.
> I am valued the more the farther from home knowledge of me has spread.

In the behaviour of his family and staff, those who heard him snoring or changed the bedlinen, there was none of the reverence of his Parisian reception, let alone his posthumous one:

> A man may appear to the world as a marvel: yet his wife and his manservant see nothing remarkable about him. Few men have been wonders to their families.

We may take this in two ways: that no one is genuinely marvellous, but that only families and staff are close enough to discern the disappointing truth. Or that many people are interesting, but that if they are too close to us in age and place, we are likely not to take them too seriously, on account of a curious bias against what is at hand.

Montaigne was not pitying himself; rather, he was using the criticism of more ambitious contemporary works as a symptom of a deleterious impulse to think that the truth always has to lie far from us, in another climate, in an ancient library, in the books of people who lived long ago. It is a question of whether access to genuinely valuable things is limited to a handful of geniuses born between the construction of the Parthenon and the sack of Rome, or whether, as Montaigne daringly proposed, they may be open to you and me as well.

A highly peculiar source of wisdom was being pointed out, more peculiar still than Pyrrho's seafaring pig, a Tupi Indian or a Gascon ploughman: the reader. If we attend properly to our experiences and learn to consider ourselves plausible candidates for an intellectual life, it is, implied Montaigne, open to all of us to arrive at insights no less profound than those in the great ancient books.

The thought is not easy. We are educated to associate virtue with submission to textual authorities, rather than with an exploration of the volumes daily transcribed within ourselves by our perceptual mechanisms. Montaigne tried to return us to ourselves:

> We know how to say, 'This is what Cicero said'; 'This is morality for Plato'; 'These are the *ipsissima verba* of Aristotle.' But what have we got to say? What judgements do we make? What are we doing? A parrot could talk as well as we do.

Parroting wouldn't be the scholar's way of describing what it takes to write a commentary. A range of arguments could show the value of producing an exegesis on the moral thought of Plato or the ethics of Cicero. Montaigne emphasized the cowardice and tedium in the activity instead. There is little skill in secondary works ('Invention takes incomparably higher precedence over quotation'), the difficulty is technical, a matter of patience and a quiet library. Furthermore, many of the books which academic tradition encourages us to parrot are not fascinating in themselves. They are accorded a central place in the syllabus because they are the work of prestigious authors, while many equally or far more valid themes languish because no grand intellectual authority ever elucidated them. The relation of art to reality has long been considered a serious philosophical topic, in part because Plato first raised it; the relation of shyness to personal appearance has not, in part because it did not attract the attention of any ancient philosopher.

In light of this unnatural respect for tradition, Montaigne thought it worth while to admit to his readers that, in truth, he thought Plato could be limited and dull:

> Will the licence of our age excuse my audacious sacrilege in thinking that [his] *Dialogues* drag slowly along stifling his matter, and in lamenting the time spent on those long useless preparatory discussions by a man who had so many better things to say?

(A relief to come upon this thought in Montaigne, one prestigious writer lending credence to timid, silent suspicions of another.) As for Cicero, there was no need even to apologize before attacking:

> His introductory passages, his definitions, his sub-divisions and his etymologies eat up most of his work ... If I spend an hour reading him (which is a lot for me) and then recall what pith and substance I have got out of him, most of the time I find nothing but wind.

If scholars paid such attention to the classics, it was, suggested Montaigne, from a vainglorious wish to be thought intelligent through association with prestigious names. The result for the reading public was a mountain of very learned, very unwise books:

> There are more books on books than on any other subject: all we do is gloss each other. All is a-swarm with commentaries: of authors there is a dearth.

But interesting ideas are, Montaigne insisted, to be found in every life. However modest our stories, we can derive greater insights from ourselves than from all the books of old:

> Were I a good scholar, I would find enough in my own experience to make me wise. Whoever recalls to mind his last bout of anger . . .
> sees the ugliness of this passion better than in Aristotle. Anyone who recalls the ills he has undergone, those which have threatened him and the trivial incidents which have moved him from one condition to another, makes himself thereby ready for future mutations and the exploring of his condition. Even the life of Caesar is less exemplary for us than our own; a life whether

imperial or plebeian is always a life affected by everything that can happen to a man.
Only an intimidating scholarly culture makes us think otherwise:
We are richer than we think, each one of us.

We may all arrive at wise ideas if we cease to think of ourselves as so unsuited to the task because we aren't 2,000 years old, aren't interested in Plato's dialogues and live quietly in the country:
You can attach the whole of moral philosophy to a commonplace private life just as well as to one of richer stuff.

It was perhaps to bring the point home that Montaigne offered so much information on exactly how commonplace and private his own life had been – why he wanted to tell us:
That he didn't like apples:
I am not overfond . . . of any fruit except melons.
That he had a complex relationship with radishes:
I first of all found that radishes agreed with me; then they did not; now they do again.
That he practised the most advanced dental hygiene:
My teeth . . . have always been exceedingly good . . . Since boyhood I learned to rub them on my napkin, both on waking up and before and after meals.
That he ate too fast:
In my haste I often bite my tongue and occasionally my fingers.
And liked wiping his mouth:
I could dine easily enough without a tablecloth, but I feel very uncomfortable dining without a clean napkin . . . I regret that we have not continued along the lines of the fashion started by our kings, changing napkins likes plates with each course.
Trivia, perhaps, but symbolic reminders that there was a thinking 'I' behind his book, that a moral philosophy had issued – and so could issue again – from an ordinary, fruit-resistant soul.

There is no need to be discouraged if, from the outside, we look nothing like those who have ruminated in the past.

Cicero 106–43 BC

In Montaigne's redrawn portrait of the adequate, semi-rational human being, it is possible to speak no Greek, fart, change one's mind after a meal, get bored with books, know none of the ancient philosophers and mistake Scipios.

A virtuous, ordinary life, striving for wisdom but never far from folly, is achievement enough.

V

Consolation for a Broken Heart

I

For the griefs of love, he may be the finest among philosophers:

The Life, 1788–1860

1788 Arthur Schopenhauer is born in Danzig. In later years, he looks back on the event with regret: 'We can regard our life as a uselessly disturbing episode in the blissful repose of nothingness.' 'Human existence must be a kind of error,' he specifies, 'it may be said of it, "It is bad today and every day it will get worse, until the worst of all happens." ' Schopenhauer's father Heinrich, a wealthy merchant, and his mother Johanna, a dizzy socialite twenty years her husband's junior, take little interest in their son, who grows into one of the greatest pessimists in the history of philosophy: 'Even as a child of six, my parents, returning from a walk one evening, found me in deep despair.'

Heinrich Schopenhauer   Johanna Schopenhauer

1803–5   After the apparent suicide of his father (discovered floating in a canal beside the family warehouse), the seventeen-year-old
Schopenhauer is left with a fortune that ensures he will never
have to work. The thought affords no comfort. He later recalls:
'In my seventeenth year, without any learned school education, I
was gripped by the *misery of life* as Buddha was in his youth
when he saw sickness, old age, pain and death. The truth . . . was
that this world could not have been the work of an all-loving
Being, but rather that of a devil, who had brought creatures into
existence in order to delight in the sight of their sufferings; to
this the data pointed, and the belief that it is so won the upper
hand.'

Schopenhauer is sent to London to learn English at a boarding-
school, Eagle House in Wimbledon. After receiving a letter from
him, his friend Lorenz Meyer replies, 'I am sorry that your stay in
England has induced you to hate the entire *nation.*' Despite the
hatred, he acquires an almost perfect command of the language,
and is often mistaken for an Englishman in conversation.

Eagle House School, Wimbledon

Schopenhauer travels through France, he visits the city of Nîmes, to which, 1,800 or so years before, Roman engineers had piped water across the majestic Pont du Gard to ensure that citizens would always have enough water to bathe in. Schopenhauer is unimpressed by what he sees of the Roman remains: 'These traces soon lead one's thoughts to the thousands of long-decomposed humans.'

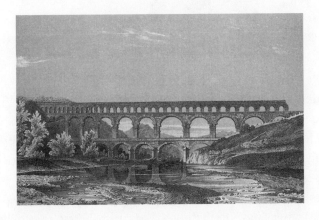

Schopenhauer's mother complains of her son's passion for 'pondering on human misery'.

1809–1811   Schopenhauer studies at the university of Göttingen and decides to become a philosopher: 'Life is a sorry business, I have resolved to spend it reflecting upon it.'

On an excursion to the countryside, a male friend suggests they should attempt to meet women. Schopenhauer quashes the plan, arguing that 'life is so short, questionable and evanescent that it is not worth the trouble of major effort.'

Schopenhauer as a young man

1813   He visits his mother in Weimar. Johanna Schopenhauer has befriended the town's most famous resident, Johann Wolfgang von Goethe, who visits her regularly (and likes talking with Sophie, Johanna's housemaid, and Adele, Arthur's younger sister). After an initial meeting, Schopenhauer describes Goethe as 'serene, sociable, obliging, friendly: praised be his name for ever and ever!' Goethe reports, 'Young Schopenhauer appeared to me to be a strange and interesting young man.' Arthur's feelings for the writer are never wholly reciprocated. When the philosopher leaves Weimar, Goethe composes a couplet for him:

Willst du dich des Lebens freuen,
So musst der Welt du Werth verleihen.
If you wish to draw pleasure out of life,
You must attach value to the world.

Schopenhauer is unimpressed, and in his notebook beside Goethe's tip, appends a quotation from Chamfort: *'Il vaut mieux laisser les hommes pour ce qu'ils sont, que les prendre pour ce qu'ils ne sont pas.'* (Better to accept men for what they are, than to take them to be what they are not.)

1814–15 Schopenhauer moves to Dresden and writes a thesis (*On the Fourfold Root of the Principle of Sufficient Reason*). He has few friends and enters into conversations with reduced expectations: 'Sometimes I speak to men and women just as a little girl speaks to her doll. She knows, of course, that the doll does not understand her, but she creates for herself the joy of communication through a pleasant and conscious self-deception.' He becomes a regular in an Italian tavern, which serves his favourite meats – Venetian salami, truffled sausage and Parma ham.

1818 He finishes *The World as Will and Representation*, which he knows to be a masterpiece. It explains his lack of friends: 'A man of genius can hardly be sociable, for what dialogues could indeed be so intelligent and entertaining as his own monologues?'

1818–19 To celebrate the completion of his book, Schopenhauer travels to Italy. He delights in art, nature and the climate, though his mood remains fragile: 'We should always be mindful of the fact that no man is ever very far from the state in which he would readily want to seize a sword or poison in order to bring his existence to an end; and those who are far from believing this could easily be convinced of the opposite by an accident, an illness, a violent change of fortune – or of the weather.' He visits Florence, Rome, Naples and Venice and meets a number of attractive women at receptions: 'I was very fond of them – if only they would have had me.' Rejection helps to inspire a view that: 'Only the male intellect, clouded by the sexual impulse, could call the undersized, narrow-shouldered, broad-hipped, and short-legged sex the fair sex.'

1819 *The World as Will and Representation* is published. It sells 230 copies. 'Every life history is a history of suffering'; 'If only I could get rid of the illusion of regarding the generation of vipers and toads as my equals, it would be a great help to me.'

1820 Schopenhauer attempts to gain a university post in philosophy in Berlin. He offers lectures on 'The whole of philosophy, i.e. the theory of the essence of the world and of the human mind.' Five students attend. In a nearby building, his rival, Hegel, can be heard lecturing to an audience of 300. Schopenhauer assesses Hegel's philosophy: '[I]ts fundamental ideas are the absurdest fancy, a world turned upside down, a philosophical buffoonery . . . its contents being the hollowest and most senseless display of words ever lapped up by blockheads, and its presentation . . . being the most repulsive and nonsensical gibberish, recalling the rantings of a bedlamite.' The beginnings of disenchantment with academia: 'That one can be serious about philosophy has as a rule not occurred to anyone, least of all to a lecturer on philosophy, just as no one as a rule believes less in Christianity than does the Pope.'

1821 Schopenhauer falls in love with Caroline Medon, a nineteen-year-old singer. The relationship lasts intermittently for ten years, but Schopenhauer has no wish to formalize the arrangement: 'To marry means to do everything possible to become an object of disgust to each other.' He nevertheless has fond thoughts of polygamy: 'Of the many advantages of polygamy, one is that the husband would not come into such close contact with his in-laws, the fear of which at present prevents innumerable marriages. Ten mothers-in-law instead of one!'

1822 Travels to Italy for a second time (Milan, Florence, Venice). Before setting out, he asks his friend Friedrich Osann to look out for 'any mention of me in books, journals, literary periodicals and such like.' Osann does not find the task time-consuming.

1825 Having failed as an academic, Schopenhauer attempts to become a translator. But his offers to turn Kant into English and *Tristram Shandy* into German are rejected by publishers. He confides in a letter a melancholy wish to have 'a position in bourgeois society', though will never attain one. 'If a God has made this world, then I would not like to be the God; its misery and distress would break my heart.' Fortunately, he can rely on a comfortable sense of his own worth in darker moments: 'How often must I learn . . . that in the affairs of everyday life . . . my spirit and mind are what a telescope is in an opera-house or a cannon at a hare-hunt?'

1828 Turns forty. 'After his fortieth year,' he consoles himself, 'any man of merit . . . will hardly be free from a certain touch of misanthropy.'

1831 Now forty-three, living in Berlin, Schopenhauer thinks once again of getting married. He turns his attentions to Flora Weiss, a beautiful, spirited girl who has just turned seventeen. During a boating party, in an attempt to charm her, he smiles and offers her a bunch of white grapes. Flora later confides in her diary: 'I didn't want them. I felt revolted because old Schopenhauer had touched them, and so I let them slide, quite gently, into the water behind me.' Schopenhauer leaves Berlin in a hurry: 'Life has no genuine intrinsic worth, but is kept in motion merely by want and illusion.'

1833 He settles in a modest apartment in Frankfurt am Main, a town of some 50,000 inhabitants. He describes the city, the banking centre of continental Europe, as 'a small, stiff, internally crude, municipally puffed-up, peasant-proud nation of Abderites, whom I do not like to approach'.

His closest relationships are now with a succession of poodles, who he feels have a gentleness and humility humans lack: 'The sight of any animal immediately gives me pleasure and gladdens my heart.' He lavishes affection on these poodles, addressing them as 'Sir', and takes a keen interest in animal welfare: 'The highly intelligent dog, man's truest and most faithful friend, is put on a chain by him! Never do I see such a dog without feelings of the deepest sympathy for him and of profound indignation against his master. I think with satisfaction of a case, reported some years ago in *The Times*, where Lord X kept a large dog on a chain. One day as he was walking through the yard, he took it into his head to go and pat the dog, whereupon the animal tore his arm open from top to bottom, and quite right, too! What he meant by this was: "You are not my master, but my devil who makes a hell of my brief existence!" May this happen to all who chain up dogs.'

The philosopher adopts a rigid daily routine. He writes for three hours in the morning, plays the flute (Rossini) for an hour, then dresses in white tie for lunch in the Englischer Hof on the Rossmarkt. He has an enormous appetite, and tucks a large white napkin into his collar. He refuses to acknowledge other diners when eating, but occasionally enters into conversation over coffee. One of them describes him as 'comically disgruntled, but in fact harmless and good-naturedly gruff'.

Another reports that Schopenhauer frequently boasts of the excellent condition of his teeth as evidence that he is superior to other people, or as he puts it, superior to the 'common biped'.

After lunch, Schopenhauer retires to the library of his club, the nearby Casino Society, where he reads *The Times* – the newspaper which he feels will best inform him of the miseries of the world. In mid-afternoon, he takes a two-hour walk with his dog along the banks of the Main, muttering under his breath. In the evening, he visits the opera or the theatre, where he is often enraged by the noise of late-comers, shufflers and coughers – and writes to the authorities urging strict measures against them. Though he has read and much admires Seneca, he does not agree with the Roman philosopher's verdict on noise: 'I have for a long time been of the opinion that the quantity of noise anyone can comfortably endure is in inverse proportion to his mental powers ... The man who habitually slams doors instead of shutting them with the hand ... is not merely ill-mannered, but also coarse and narrow-minded ... We shall be quite civilized only when ... it is no longer anyone's right to cut through the consciousness of every thinking being ... by means of whistling, howling, bellowing, hammering, whip-cracking ... and so on.'

1840 He acquires a new white poodle and names her Atma, after the world-soul of the Brahmins. He is attracted to Eastern religions in general and Brahmanism in particular (he reads a few pages of the Upanishads every night). He describes Brahmins as, 'the noblest and oldest of people', and threatens to sack his cleaning lady, Margaretha Schnepp, when she disregards orders not to dust the Buddha in his study.

He spends increasing amounts of time alone. His mother worries about him: 'Two months in your room without seeing a single person, that is not good, my son, and saddens me, a man cannot and should not isolate himself in that manner.' He takes to sleeping for extended periods during the day: 'If life and existence were an enjoyable state, then everyone would reluctantly approach the unconscious state of sleep and would gladly rise from it again. But the very opposite is the case, for everyone very willingly goes to sleep and unwillingly gets up again.' He justifies his appetite for sleep by comparing himself to two of his favourite thinkers: 'Human beings require more sleep the more developed ... and the more active their brain is. Montaigne relates of himself that he had always been a heavy sleeper; that he had spent a large part of his life in sleeping; and that at an advanced age he still slept from eight to nine hours at a stretch. It is also reported of Descartes that he slept a great deal.'

1843 Schopenhauer moves to a new house in Frankfurt, number 17 Schöne Aussicht, near the river Main in the centre of town (English translation: Pretty view). He is to live in the street for the rest of his life, though in 1859, he moves to number 16 after a quarrel with his landlord over his dog.

1844 He publishes a second edition and a further volume of *The World as Will and Representation*. He remarks in the preface: 'Not to my contemporaries or my compatriots, but to mankind I consign my now complete work, confident that it will not be without value to humanity, even if this value should be recognized only tardily, as is the inevitable fate of the good in whatever form.' The work sells under 300 copies: 'Our greatest pleasure consists in being admired; but the admirers, even if there is every cause, are not very keen to express their admiration. And so the happiest man is he who has managed sincerely to admire himself, no matter how.'

1850 Atma dies. He buys a brown poodle called Butz, who becomes his favourite poodle. When a regimental band passes his house, Schopenhauer is known to stand up in the middle of conversations and put a seat by the window from which Butz can look out. The creature is referred to by the children of the neighbourhood as 'young Schopenhauer'.

1851 He publishes a selection of essays and aphorisms, *Parerga and Paralipomena*. Much to the author's surprise, the book becomes a bestseller.

1853 His fame spreads across Europe ('the comedy of fame', as he puts it). Lectures on his philosophy are offered at the universities of Bonn, Breslau and Jena. He receives fan mail. A woman from Silesia sends him a long, suggestive poem. A man from Bohemia writes to tell him he places a wreath on his portrait every day. 'After one has spent a long life in insignificance and disregard, they come at the end with drums and trumpets and think that is something' is the response, but there is also satisfaction: 'Would anyone with a great mind ever have been able to attain his goal and create a permanent and perennial work, if he had taken as his guiding star the bobbing will-o'-the-wisp of public opinion, that is to say the opinion of small minds?' Philosophically minded Frankfurters buy poodles in homage.

1859 As fame brings more attention from women, his views on them soften. From having thought them 'suited to being the nurses and teachers of our earliest childhood precisely because they themselves are childish, silly and short-sighted, in a word, big-children, their whole lives long', he now judges that they are capable of self-lessness and insight. An attractive sculptress and an admirer of his philosophy, Elizabeth Ney (a descendant of Napoleon's Maréchal), comes to Frankfurt in October and stays in his apartment for a month making a bust of him.

'She works all day at my place. When I get back from luncheon we have coffee together, we sit together on the sofa and I feel as if I were married.'

1860 Increasing ill-health suggests the end is near: 'I can bear the thought that in a short time worms will eat away my body; but the idea of philosophy professors nibbling at my philosophy makes me shudder.' At the end of September, after a walk by the banks of the Main, he returns home, complains of breathlessness and dies, still convinced that 'human existence must be a kind of error.'

∞

Such was the life of a philosopher who may offer the heart unparalleled assistance.

2

A contemporary love story
WITH SCHOPENHAUERIAN NOTES

*A*man is attempting to work on a train between Edinburgh and
London. It is early in the afternoon on a warm spring day.

*Papers and a diary are on the table before him, and a book is open on the
armrest. But the man has been unable to hold a coherent thought since
Newcastle, when a woman entered the carriage and seated herself across
the aisle. After looking impassively out of the window for a few moments,
she turned her attention to a pile of magazines. She has been reading
Vogue since Darlington. She reminds the man of a portrait by Christen
Købke of Mrs Høegh-Guldberg (though he cannot recall either of these
names), which he saw, and felt strangely moved and saddened by, in a
museum in Denmark a few years before.*

But unlike Mrs Høegh-Guldberg, she has short brown hair and wears jeans, a pair of trainers and a canary-yellow V-neck sweater over a T-shirt. He notices an incongruously large digital sports-watch on her pale, freckle-dotted wrist. He imagines running his hand through her chestnut hair, caressing the back of her neck, sliding his hand inside the sleeve of her pullover, watching her fall asleep beside him, her lips slightly agape. He imagines living with her in a house in south London, in a cherry-tree-lined street. He speculates that she may be a cellist or a graphic designer, or a doctor specializing in genetic research. His mind turns over strategies for conversation. He considers asking her for the time, for a pencil, for directions to the bathroom, for reflections on the weather, for a look at one of her magazines. He longs for a train crash, in which their carriage would be thrown into one of the vast barley-fields through which they are passing. In the chaos, he would guide her safely outside, and repair with her to a nearby tent set up by the ambulance service, where they would be offered lukewarm tea and stare into each other's eyes. Years later, they would attract interest by revealing that they had met in the tragic Edinburgh Express collision. But because the train seems disinclined to derail, and though he knows it to be louche and absurd, the man cannot help clearing his throat and leaning over to ask the angel if she might have a spare ballpoint. It feels like jumping off the side of a very high bridge.

1. Philosophers have not traditionally been impressed: the tribula-
   tions of love have appeared too childish to warrant investiga-
   tion, the subject better left to poets and hysterics. It is not for
   philosophers to speculate on hand-holding and scented letters.
   Schopenhauer was puzzled by the indifference:

   > We should be surprised that a matter that generally plays such an
   > important part in the life of man has hitherto been almost
   > entirely disregarded by philosophers, and lies before us as raw
   > and untreated material.

   The neglect seemed the result of a pompous denial of a side of
   life which violated man's rational self-image. Schopenhauer
   insisted on the awkward reality:

   > Love ... interrupts at every hour the most serious occupations,
   > and sometimes perplexes for a while even the greatest minds. It
   > does not hesitate ... to interfere with the negotiations of
   > statesmen and the investigations of the learned. It knows how to
   > slip its love-notes and ringlets even into ministerial portfolios
   > and philosophical manuscripts ... It sometimes demands the
   > sacrifice of ... health, sometimes of wealth, position and
   > happiness.

2. Like the Gascon essayist born 255 years before him, Schopenhauer was concerned with what made man – supposedly the
   most rational of all creatures – less than reasonable. There was
   a set of Montaigne's works in the library of the apartment
   at Schöne Aussicht. Schopenhauer had read how reason could
   be dethroned by a fart, a big lunch or an ingrowing toenail,
   and concurred with Montaigne's view that our minds were
   subservient to our bodies, despite our arrogant faith in the
   contrary.

3. But Schopenhauer went further. Rather than alighting on loose
   examples of the dethronement of reason, he gave a name to a
   force within us which he felt invariably had precedence over
   reason, a force powerful enough to distort all of reason's plans
   and judgements, and which he termed the will-to-life (*Wille zum*

Leben) – defined as an inherent drive within human beings to stay alive and reproduce. The will-to-life led even committed depressives to fight for survival when they were threatened by a shipwreck or grave illness. It ensured that the most cerebral, career-minded individuals would be seduced by the sight of gurgling infants, or if they remained unmoved, that they were likely to conceive a child anyway, and love it fiercely on arrival. And it was the will-to-life that drove people to lose their reason over comely passengers encountered across the aisles of long-distance trains.

4. Schopenhauer might have resented the disruption of love (it isn't easy to proffer grapes to schoolgirls); but he refused to conceive of it as either disproportionate or accidental. It was entirely commensurate with love's function:

> Why all this noise and fuss? Why all the urgency, uproar, anguish and exertion? . . . Why should such a trifle play so important a role . . .? It is no trifle that is here in question; on the contrary, the importance of the matter is perfectly in keeping with the earnestness and ardour of the effort. The ultimate aim of all love-affairs . . . is actually more important than all other aims in man's life; and therefore it is quite worthy of the profound seriousness with which everyone pursues it.

And what is the aim? Neither communion nor sexual release, understanding nor entertainment. The romantic dominates life because:

> What is decided by it is nothing less than the composition of the next generation . . . the existence and special constitution of the human race in times to come.

It is because love directs us with such force towards the second of the will-to-life's two great commands that Schopenhauer judged it the most inevitable and understandable of our obsessions.

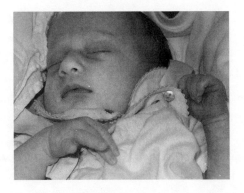

5. The fact that the continuation of the species is seldom in our minds when we ask for a phone number is no objection to the theory. We are, suggested Schopenhauer, split into conscious and unconscious selves, the unconscious governed by the will-to-life, the conscious subservient to it and unable to learn of all its plans. Rather than a sovereign entity, the conscious mind is a partially sighted servant of a dominant, child-obsessed will-to-life:

> [The intellect] does not penetrate into the secret workshop of the will's decisions. It is, of course, a confidant of the will, yet a confidant that does not get to know everything.

The intellect understands only so much as is necessary to promote reproduction – which may mean understanding very little:

> [It] remains . . . much excluded from the real resolutions and secret decisions of its own will.

An exclusion which explains how we may consciously feel nothing more than an intense desire to see someone again, while unconsciously being driven by a force aiming at the reproduction of the next generation.

Why should such deception even be necessary? Because, for Schopenhauer, we would not reliably assent to reproduce unless we first had lost our minds.

6. The analysis surely violates a rational self-image, but at least it counters suggestions that romantic love is an avoidable departure from more serious tasks, that it is forgivable for youngsters with too much time on their hands to swoon by moonlight and

sob beneath bedclothes, but that it is unnecessary and demented for their seniors to neglect their work *because they have glimpsed a face on a train.* By conceiving of love as biologically inevitable, key to the continuation of the species, Schopenhauer's theory of the will invites us to adopt a more forgiving stance towards the eccentric behaviour to which love so often makes us subject.

*T*he man and woman are seated at a window-table in a Greek restaurant in north London. A bowl of olives lies between them, but neither can think of a way to remove the stones with requisite dignity and so they are left untouched.

She had not been carrying a ballpoint on her, but had offered him a pencil. After a pause, she said how much she hated long train-journeys, a superfluous remark which had given him the slender encouragement he needed. She was not a cellist, nor a graphic designer, rather a lawyer specializing in corporate finance in a city firm. She was originally from Newcastle, but had been living in London for the past eight years. By the time the train pulled into Euston, he had obtained a phone number and an assent to a suggestion of dinner.

   A waiter arrives to take their order. She asks for a salad and the swordfish. She has come directly from work, and is wearing a light-grey suit and the same watch as before.

They begin to talk. She explains that at weekends, her favourite activity is rock-climbing. She started at school, and has since been on expeditions to France, Spain and Canada. She describes the thrill of hanging hundreds of feet above a valley floor, and camping in the high mountains, where in the morning, icicles have formed inside the tent. Her dinner companion feels dizzy on the second floor of apartment buildings. Her other passion is dancing, she loves the energy and sense of freedom. When she can, she stays up all night. He favours proximity to a bed by eleven thirty. They talk of work. She has been involved in a patent case. A kettle designer from Frankfurt has alleged copyright infringement against a British company. The company is liable under section 60,1,a of the Patents Act of 1977.

He does not follow the lengthy account of a forthcoming case, but is convinced of her high intelligence and their superlative compatibility.

1. One of the most profound mysteries of love is 'Why him?', and 'Why her?' Why, of all the possible candidates, did our desire settle so strongly on this creature, why did we come to treasure them above all others when their dinner conversation was not always the most enlightening, nor their habits the most suitable? And why, despite good intentions, were we unable to develop a sexual interest in certain others, who were perhaps objectively as attractive and might have been more convenient to live with?

2. The choosiness did not surprise Schopenhauer. We are not free to fall in love with everyone because we cannot produce healthy children with everyone. Our will-to-life drives us towards people who will raise our chances of producing beautiful and intelligent offspring, and repulses us away from those who lower these same chances. Love is nothing but the conscious manifestation of the will-to-life's discovery of an ideal co-parent:

The moment when [two people] begin to love each other – *to fancy each other*, as the very apposite English expression has it – is actually to be regarded as the very first formation of a new individual.

In initial meetings, beneath the quotidian patter, the unconscious of both parties will assess whether a healthy child could one day result from intercourse:

There is something quite peculiar to be found in the deep, unconscious seriousness with which two young people of the opposite sex regard each other when they meet for the first time, the searching and penetrating glance they cast at each other, the careful inspection all the features and parts of their respective persons have to undergo. This scrutiny and examination is the meditation of the genius of the species concerning the individual possible through these two.

3. And what is the will-to-life seeking through such examination? Evidence of healthy children. The will-to-life must ensure that the next generation will be psychologically and physiologically fit enough to survive in a hazardous world, and so it seeks that children be well-proportioned in limb (neither too short nor too tall, too fat nor too thin), and stable of mind (neither too timid nor too reckless, neither too cold nor too emotional, etc.).

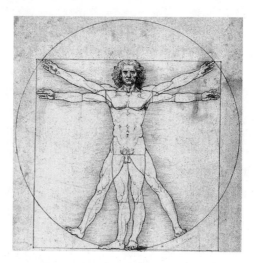

Since our parents made errors in their courtships, we are unlikely to be ideally balanced ourselves. We have typically come out too tall, too masculine, too feminine; our noses are large, our chins small. If such imbalances were allowed to persist, or were aggravated, the human race would, within a short time, founder in oddity. The will-to-life must therefore push us towards people who can, on account of their imperfections, cancel out our own (a large nose combined with a button nose promises a perfect nose), and hence help us restore physical and psychological balance in the next generation:

> Everyone endeavours to eliminate through the other individual his own weaknesses, defects, and deviations from the type, lest they be perpetuated or even grow into complete abnormalities in the child which will be produced.

The theory of neutralization gave Schopenhauer confidence in predicting pathways of attraction. Short women will fall in love with tall men, but rarely tall men with tall women (their unconscious fearing the production of giants). Feminine men who don't like sport will often be drawn to boyish women who have short hair (and wear sturdy watches):

> The neutralization of the two individualities . . . requires that the particular degree of *his* manliness shall correspond exactly to the particular degree of *her* womanliness, so that the one-sidedness of each exactly cancels that of the other.

4. Unfortunately, the theory of attraction led Schopenhauer to a conclusion so bleak, it may be best if readers about to be married left the next few paragraphs unread in order not to have to rethink their plans; namely, that a person who is highly suitable for our child is almost never (though we cannot realize it at the time because we have been blindfolded by the will-to-life) very suitable for us.

'That convenience and passionate love should go hand in hand is the rarest stroke of good fortune,' observed Schopenhauer. The lover who saves our child from having an enormous chin or an effeminate temperament is seldom the person who will make us happy over a lifetime. The pursuit of personal happiness and the production of healthy children are two radically contrasting projects, which love maliciously confuses us into thinking of as one for a requisite number of years. We should not be surprised by marriages between people who would never have been friends:

> Love ... casts itself on persons who, apart from the sexual relation, would be hateful, contemptible, and even abhorrent to the lover. But the will of the species is so much more powerful than that of the individual, that the lover shuts his eyes to all the qualities repugnant to him, overlooks everything, misjudges everything, and binds himself for ever to the object of his passion. He is thus completely infatuated by that delusion, which vanishes as soon as the will of the species is satisfied, and leaves behind a detested partner for life. Only from this is it possible to explain why we often see very rational, and even eminent, men tied to termagants and matrimonial fiends, and cannot conceive how they could have made such a choice ... A man in love may even clearly recognize and bitterly feel in his bride the intolerable faults of temperament and character which promise him a life of misery, and yet not be frightened away ... for ultimately he seeks not *his* interest, but that of a third person who has yet to come into existence, although he is involved in the delusion that what he seeks is his own interest.

The will-to-life's ability to further its own ends rather than our happiness may, Schopenhauer's theory implies, be sensed with particular clarity in the lassitude and tristesse that frequently befall couples immediately after love-making:

> Has it not been observed how *illico post coitum cachinnus auditur Diaboli?* (Directly after copulation the devil's laughter is heard.)

So one day, a boyish woman and a girlish man will approach the altar with motives neither they, nor anyone (save a smattering of Schopenhauerians at the reception), will have fathomed.

Only later, when the will's demands are assuaged and a robust boy is kicking a ball around a suburban garden, will the ruse be discovered. The couple will part or pass dinners in hostile silence. Schopenhauer offered us a choice –

It seems as if, in making a marriage, either the individual or the interest of the species must come off badly

– though he left us in little doubt as to the superior capacity of the species to guarantee its interests:

The coming generation is provided for at the expense of the present.

The man pays for dinner and asks, with studied casualness, if it might be an idea to repair to his flat for a drink. She smiles and stares at the floor. Under the table, she is folding a paper napkin into ever smaller squares. 'That would be lovely, it really would,' she says, 'but I have to get up very early to catch a flight to Frankfurt for this meeting. Five thirty or, like, even earlier. Maybe another time though. It would be lovely. Really, it would.' Another smile. The napkin disintegrates under pressure.

Despair is alleviated by a promise that she will call from Germany, and that they must meet again soon, perhaps on the very day of her return. But there is no call until late on the appointed day, when she rings from a booth at Frankfurt airport. In the background are crowds and metallic voices announcing the departure of flights to the Orient. She tells him she can see huge planes out of the window and that this place is like hell.

She says that the fucking Lufthansa flight has been delayed, that she will try to get a seat on another airline but that he shouldn't wait. There follows a pause before the worst is confirmed. Things are a little complicated in her life right now really, she goes on, she doesn't quite know what she wants, but she knows she needs space and some time, and if it is all right with him, she will be the one to call once her head is a little clearer.

1. The philosopher might have offered unflattering explanations of why we fall in love, but there was consolation for rejection – the consolation of knowing that our pain is normal. We should not feel confused by the enormity of the upset that can ensue from only a few days of hope. It would be unreasonable if a force powerful enough to push us towards child-rearing could – if it failed in its aim – vanish without devastation. Love could not induce us to take on the burden of propagating the species without promising us the greatest happiness we could imagine. To be shocked at how deeply rejection hurts is to ignore what acceptance involves. We must never allow our suffering to be compounded by suggestions that there is something odd in suffering so deeply. There would be something amiss if we didn't.

2. What is more, we are not inherently unlovable. There is nothing wrong with us *per se*. Our characters are not repellent, nor our faces abhorrent. The union collapsed because we were unfit to produce a balanced child *with one particular person*. There is no need to hate ourselves. One day we will come across someone who can find us wonderful and who will feel exceptionally natural and open with us (because our chin and their chin make a desirable combination from the will-to-life's point of view).

3. We should in time learn to forgive our rejectors. The break-up was not their choice. In every clumsy attempt by one person to inform another that they need more space or time, that they are reluctant to commit or are afraid of intimacy, the rejector is striving to intellectualize an essentially unconscious negative

verdict formulated by the will-to-life. Their reason may have had an appreciation of our qualities, their will-to-life did not and told them so in a way that brooked no argument – by draining them of sexual interest in us. If they were seduced away by people less intelligent than we are, we should not condemn them for shallowness. We should remember, as Schopenhauer explains, that:

> What is looked for in marriage is not intellectual entertainment,
> but the procreation of children.

4. We should respect the edict from nature against procreation that every rejection contains, as we might respect a flash of lightning or a lava flow – an event terrible but mightier than ourselves. We should draw consolation from the thought that a lack of love:

> between a man and a woman is the announcement that what
> they might produce would only be a badly organized, unhappy
> being, wanting in harmony in itself.

We might have been happy with our beloved, but nature was not – a greater reason to surrender our grip on love.

For a time, the man is beset by melancholy. At the weekend, he takes a walk in Battersea Park, and sits on a bench overlooking the Thames. He has with him a paperback edition of Goethe's The Sorrows of Young Werther, *first published in Leipzig in 1774.*

There are couples pushing prams and leading young children by the hand. A little girl in a blue dress covered in chocolate, points up to a plane descending towards Heathrow. 'Daddy, is God in there?' she asks, but Daddy is in a hurry and in a mood, and picks her up and says he doesn't know, as though he had been asked for directions. A four-year-old boy drives his tricycle into a shrub and wails for his mother, who has just shut her eyes on a rug spread on a tattered patch of grass. She requests that her husband assist the child. He gruffly replies that it is her turn. She snaps that it is his. He says nothing. She says he's crap and stands up. An elderly couple on an adjacent bench silently share an egg-and-cress sandwich.

1. Schopenhauer asks us not to be surprised by the misery. We should not ask for a point to being alive, in a couple or a parent.
2. There were many works of natural science in Schopenhauer's library – among them William Kirby and William Spence's *Introduction to Entomology*, François Huber's *Des Abeilles* and Cadet de Vaux's *De la taupe, de ses moeurs, de ses habitudes et des moyens de la détruire*. The philosopher read of ants, beetles, bees, flies, grasshoppers, moles and migratory birds, and observed, with compassion and puzzlement, how all these creatures displayed an ardent, senseless commitment to life. He felt particular sympathy for the mole, a stunted monstrosity dwelling in damp narrow corridors, who rarely saw the light of day and whose offspring looked like gelatinous worms – but who still did everything in its power to survive and perpetuate itself:

   > To dig strenuously with its enormous shovel-paws is the business of its whole life; permanent night surrounds it; it has its embryo eyes merely to avoid the light . . . what does it attain by this course of life that is full of trouble and devoid of pleasure? . . . The cares and troubles of life are out of all proportion to the yield or profit from it.

   Every creature on earth seemed to Schopenhauer to be equally committed to an equally meaningless existence:

Contemplate the restless industry of
wretched little ants . . . the life of most
insects is nothing but a restless labour
for preparing nourishment and dwelling for the future offspring that will
come from their eggs. After the offspring have consumed the nourishment and have turned into the
chrysalis stage, they enter into life
merely to begin the same task again
from the beginning . . . we cannot
help but ask what comes of all of this
. . . there is nothing to show but the

satisfaction of hunger and sexual passion, and . . . a little momen-
tary gratification . . . now and then, between . . . endless needs
and exertions.

3. The philosopher did not have to spell out the parallels. We
   pursue love affairs, chat in cafés with prospective partners and
   have children, with as much choice in the matter as moles and
   ants – and are rarely any happier.

4. He did not mean to depress us, rather to free us from expectations which inspire bitterness. It is consoling, when love has let

us down, to hear that happiness was never part of the plan. The darkest thinkers may, paradoxically, be the most cheering:

> There is only one inborn error, and that is the notion that we exist in order to be happy . . . So long as we persist in this inborn error . . . the world seems to us full of contradictions. For at every step, in great things and small, we are bound to experience that the world and life are certainly not arranged for the purpose of maintaining a happy existence . . . hence the countenances of almost all elderly persons wear the expression of what is called *disappointment*.

They would never have grown so disappointed if only they had entered love with the correct expectations:

> What disturbs and renders unhappy . . . the age of youth . . . is the hunt for happiness on the firm assumption that it must be met with in life. From this arises the constantly deluded hope and so also dissatisfaction. Deceptive images of a vague happiness of our dreams hover before us in capriciously selected shapes and we search in vain for their original . . . Much would have been gained if through timely advice and instruction young people could have had eradicated from their minds the erroneous notion that the world has a great deal to offer them.

3

We do have one advantage over moles. We may have to fight for survival and hunt for partners and have children as they do, but we can in addition go to the theatre, the opera and the concert hall, and in bed in the evenings, we can read novels, philosophy and epic poems – and it is in these activities that Schopenhauer located a supreme source of relief from the demands of the will-to-life. What we encounter in works of art and philosophy are objective versions of our own pains and struggles, evoked and defined in sound, language or image. Artists and philosophers not only show us what we have felt, they present our experiences more poignantly and intelligently than we have been able; they give shape to aspects of our lives that we recognize as our own, yet could never have understood so clearly on our own. They explain our condition to us, and thereby help us to be less lonely with, and confused by it. We may be obliged to continue burrowing underground, but through creative works, we can at least acquire moments of insight into our woes, which spare us feelings of alarm and isolation (even persecution) at being afflicted by them. In their different ways, art and philosophy help us, in Schopenhauer's words, to turn pain into knowledge.

The philosopher admired his mother's friend Johann Wolfgang von Goethe because he had turned so many of the pains of love into knowledge, most famously in the novel he had published at the age of twenty-five, and which had made his name throughout Europe. *The Sorrows of Young Werther* described the unrequited love felt by a particular young man for a particular young woman (the charming Lotte, who shared Werther's taste for *The Vicar of Wakefield* and wore white dresses with pink ribbons at the sleeves), but it simultaneously described the love affairs of thousands of its readers (Napoleon was said to have read the novel nine times). The greatest works of art speak to us without knowing of us. As Schopenhauer put it:

> The ... poet takes from life that which is quite particular and individual, and describes it accurately in its individuality; but in this way he reveals the whole of human existence ... though he appears to be concerned with the particular, he is actually concerned with that which is everywhere and at all times. From this it arises that sentences, especially of the dramatic poets, even without being general apophthegms, find frequent application in real life.

Goethe's readers not only *recognized* themselves in *The Sorrows of Young Werther*, they also *understood* themselves better as a result, for Goethe had clarified a range of the awkward, evanescent moments of love, moments that his readers would previously have lived through, though would not necessarily have fathomed. He laid bare certain laws of love, what Schopenhauer termed essential 'Ideas' of romantic psychology. He had, for example, perfectly captured the apparently kind – yet infinitely cruel – manner with which the person who does not love deals with the one who does. Late in the novel, tortured by his feelings, Werther breaks down in front of Lotte:

> 'Lotte' he cried, 'I shall never see you again!' – 'Why ever not?' she replied: 'Werther, you may and must see us again, but do be less agitated in your manner. Oh, why did you have to be born with this intense spirit, this uncontrollable passion for everything you are close to! I implore you,' she went on, taking his hand, 'be calmer. Think of the many joys your spirit, your knowledge and your gifts afford you!'

We need not have lived in Germany in the second half of the eighteenth century to appreciate what is involved. There are fewer stories than there are people on earth, the plots repeated ceaselessly while the names and backdrops alter. 'The essence of art is that its one case applies to thousands,' knew Schopenhauer.

In turn, there is consolation in realizing that our case is *only* one of thousands. Schopenhauer made two trips to Florence, in 1818 and again in 1822. He is likely to have visited the Brancacci chapel in Santa Maria del Carmine, in which Masaccio had painted a series of frescos between 1425 and 1426.

The distress of Adam and Eve at leaving paradise is not theirs alone. In the faces and posture of the two figures, Masaccio has captured the essence of distress, the very Idea of distress, his fresco a universal symbol of our fallibility and fragility. We have all been expelled from the heavenly garden.

But by reading a tragic tale of love, a rejected suitor raises himself above his own situation; he is no longer one man suffering alone, singly and confusedly, he is part of a vast body of human beings who have throughout time fallen in love with other humans in the agonizing drive to propagate the species. His suffering loses a little of its sting, it grows more comprehensible, less of an individual curse. Of a person who can achieve such objectivity, Schopenhauer remarks:

> In the course of his own life and in its misfortunes, he will look less at his own individual lot than at the lot of mankind as a whole, and accordingly will conduct himself . . . more as a *knower* than as a
> . *sufferer.*

We must, between periods of digging in the dark, endeavour always to transform our tears into knowledge.

VI

Consolation for Difficulties

Few philosophers have thought highly of feeling wretched. A wise life has traditionally been associated with an attempt to reduce suffering: anxiety, despair, anger, self-contempt and heartache.

2

Then again, pointed out Friedrich Nietzsche, the majority of philosophers have always been 'cabbage-heads'. 'It is my fate to have to be the first *decent* human being,' he recognized with a degree of embarrassment in the autumn of 1888. 'I have a terrible fear that I shall one day be pronounced *holy*'; and he set the date somewhere around the dawn of the third millennium: 'Let us assume that people will be *allowed* to read [my work] in about the year 2000.' He was sure they would enjoy it when they did:

> It seems to me that to take a book of mine into his hands is one of
> the rarest distinctions that anyone can confer upon himself. I even
> assume that he removes his shoes when he does so – not to speak of
> boots.

A distinction because, alone among the cabbage-heads, Nietzsche had realized that difficulties of every sort were to be welcomed by those seeking fulfilment:

> You want if possible – and there is no madder 'if possible' – *to*
> *abolish suffering*; and we? – it really does seem that *we* would rather
> increase it and make it worse than it has ever been!

Though punctilious in sending his best wishes to friends, Nietzsche knew in his heart what they needed:

To those human beings who are of any concern to me I wish
suffering, desolation, sickness, ill-treatment, indignities – I wish that
they should not remain unfamiliar with profound self-contempt,
the torture of self-mistrust, the wretchedness of the vanquished.
Which helped to explain why his work amounted to, even if he said
so himself:

The greatest gift that [mankind] has ever been given.

3

We should not be frightened by appearances.

*In the eyes of people who are seeing us for the first time . . . usually we are
nothing more than a single individual trait which leaps to the eye and
determines the whole impression we make. Thus the gentlest and most
reasonable of men can, if he wears a large moustache . . . usually be seen as no
more than the appurtenance of a large moustache, that is to say a military
type, easily angered and occasionally violent – and as such he will be treated.*

4

He had not always thought so well of difficulty. For his initial views, he had been indebted to a philosopher he had discovered at the age of twenty-one as a student at Leipzig University. In the autumn of 1865, in a second-hand bookshop in Leipzig's Blumen-gasse, he had by chance picked up an edition of *The World as Will and Representation*, whose author had died five years previously in an apartment in Frankfurt 300 kilometres to the west:

> I took [Schopenhauer's book] in my hand as something totally unfamiliar and turned the pages. I don't know which daimon was whispering to me: 'Take this book home.' In any case, it happened, which was contrary to my custom of otherwise never rushing into buying a book. Back at the house I threw myself into the corner of a sofa with my new treasure, and began to let that dynamic, dismal genius work on me. Each line cried out with renunciation, negation, resignation.

The older man changed the younger one's life. The essence of philosophical wisdom was, Schopenhauer explained, Aristotle's remark in the *Nicomachean Ethics*:

> The prudent man strives for freedom from pain, not pleasure.

The priority for all those seeking contentment was to recognize the impossibility of fulfilment and so to avoid the troubles and anxiety that we typically encounter in its pursuit:

> [We should] direct our aim not to what is pleasant and agreeable in life, but to the avoidance, as far as possible, of its numberless evils
> ... The happiest lot is that of the man who has got through life without any very great pain, bodily or mental.

When he next wrote home to his widowed mother and his nine-teen-year-old sister in Naumburg, Nietzsche replaced the usual reports on his diet and the progress of his studies with a summary of his new philosophy of renunciation and resignation:

> We know that life consists of suffering, that the harder we try to

enjoy it, the more enslaved we are by it, and so we [should] discard
the goods of life and practise abstinence.

It sounded strange to his mother, who wrote back explaining that
she didn't like 'that kind of display or that kind of opinion so much
as a proper letter, full of news', and advised her son to entrust his
heart to God and to make sure he was eating properly.

But Schopenhauer's influence did not subside. Nietzsche began
to live cautiously. Sex figured prominently in a list he drew up
under the heading 'Delusions of the Individual'. During his military
service in Naumburg, he positioned a photograph of Schopenhauer
on his desk, and in difficult moments cried out, 'Schopenhauer,
help!' At the age of twenty-four, on taking up the Chair of Classical
Philology at Basle University, he was drawn into the intimate circle
of Richard and Cosima Wagner through a common love of the
pessimistic, prudent sage of Frankfurt.

5

Then, after more than a decade of attachment, in the autumn of
1876, Nietzsche travelled to Italy and underwent a radical change of
mind. He had accepted an invitation from Malwida von
Meysenbug, a wealthy middle-aged enthusiast of the arts, to spend
a few months with her and a group of friends in a villa in Sorrento
on the Bay of Naples.

'I never saw him so lively. He laughed aloud from sheer joy,' reported Malwida of Nietzsche's first response to the Villa Rubinacci, which stood on a leafy avenue on the edge of Sorrento. From the living room there were views over the bay, the island of Ischia and Mount Vesuvius, and in front of the house, a small garden with fig and orange trees, cypresses and grape arbours led down to the sea.

The house guests went swimming, and visited Pompeii, Vesuvius, Capri and the Greek temples at Paestum. At mealtimes, they ate light dishes prepared with olive oil, and in the evenings, read together in the living room: Jacob Burckhardt's lectures on Greek civilization, Montaigne, La Rochefoucauld, Vauvenargues, La Bruyère, Stendhal, Goethe's ballad *Die Braut von Korinth*, and his play *Die natürliche Tochter*, Herodotus, Thucydides, and Plato's *Laws* (though, perhaps spurred on by Montaigne's confessions of distaste, Nietzsche grew irritated with the latter: 'The Platonic dialogue, that dreadfully self-satisfied and childish kind of dialectics, can only have a stimulating effect if one has never read any good Frenchmen . . . Plato is boring').

And as he swam in the Mediterranean, ate food cooked in olive oil rather than butter, breathed warm air and read Montaigne and Stendhal ('These little things – nutriment, place, climate, recreation, the whole casuistry of selfishness – are beyond all conception of greater importance than anything that has been considered of importance hitherto'), Nietzsche gradually changed his philosophy of pain and pleasure, and with it, his perspective on difficulty. Watching the sun set over the Bay of Naples at the end of October 1876, he was infused with a new, quite un-Schopenhauerian faith in existence. He felt that he had been old at the beginning of his life, and shed tears at the thought that he had been saved at the last moment.

6

He made a formal announcement of his conversion in a letter to Cosima Wagner at the end of 1876: 'Would you be amazed if I confess something that has gradually come about, but which has more or less suddenly entered my consciousness: a disagreement with Schopenhauer's teaching? On virtually all general propositions I am not on his side.'

One of these propositions being that, because fulfilment is an illusion, the wise must devote themselves to avoiding pain rather than seeking pleasure, living quietly, as Schopenhauer counselled, 'in a small fireproof room' – advice that now struck Nietzsche as both timid and untrue, a perverse attempt to dwell, as he was to put it pejoratively several years later, 'hidden in forests like shy deer'. Fulfilment was to be reached not by avoiding pain, but by recognizing its role as a natural, inevitable step on the way to reaching anything good.

7

What had, besides the food and the air, helped to change Nietzsche's outlook was his reflection on the few individuals throughout history who appeared genuinely to have known fulfilled lives; individuals who could fairly have been described – to use one of the most contested terms in the Nietzschean lexicon – as *Übermenschen*.

The notoriety and absurdity of the word owe less to Nietzsche's own philosophy than to his sister Elisabeth's subsequent enchantment with National Socialism ('that vengeful anti-Semitic goose', as Friedrich described her long before she shook the Führer's hand), and the unwitting decision by Nietzsche's earliest Anglo-Saxon translators to bequeath to the *Übermensch* the name of a legendary cartoon hero.

Hitler greeting Elisabeth Nietzsche
in Weimar, October 1935

But Nietzsche's *Übermenschen* had little to do with either airborne
aces or fascists. A better indication of their identity came in a passing remark in a letter to his mother and sister:

> Really, there is nobody living about whom I care *much*. The people
> I like have been dead for a long, long time – for example, the Abbé
> Galiani, or Henri Beyle, or Montaigne.

He could have added another hero, Johann Wolfgang von Goethe.
These four men were perhaps the richest clues for what Nietzsche
came in his maturity to understand by a fulfilled life.

They had much in common. They were curious, artistically gifted,
and sexually vigorous. Despite their dark sides, they laughed, and
many of them danced, too; they were drawn to 'gentle sunlight,
bright and buoyant air, southerly vegetation, the breath of the
sea [and] fleeting meals of flesh, fruit and eggs'. Several of them
had a gallows humour close to Nietzsche's own – a joyful, wicked
laughter arising from pessimistic hinterlands. They had explored
their possibilities, they possessed what Nietzsche called 'life', which
suggested courage, ambition, dignity, strength of character,

humour and independence (and a parallel absence of sanctimoniousness, conformity, resentment and prissiness).

Montaigne (1533–92)

Abbé Galiani (1728–87)

Goethe (1749–1832)

Stendhal/Henri Beyle (1783–1842)

They had been involved in the world. Montaigne had been mayor of Bordeaux for two terms and journeyed across Europe on horseback. The Neapolitan Abbé Galiani had been Secretary to the Embassy in Paris and written works on money supply and grain distribution (which Voltaire praised for combining the wit of Molière and the intelligence of Plato). Goethe had worked for a decade as a civil servant in the Court in Weimar; he had proposed reforms in agriculture, industry and poor relief, undertaken diplomatic missions and twice had audiences with Napoleon.

On his visit to Italy in 1787, he had seen the Greek temples at Paestum and made three ascents of Mount Vesuvius, coming close enough to the crater to dodge eruptions of stone and ash.

Nietzsche called him 'magnificent', 'the last German I hold in reverence': 'He made use of ... practical activity ... he did not divorce himself from life but immersed himself in it . . . [he] took as much as possible upon himself . . . What he wanted was totality; he fought against the disjunction of reason, sensuality, feeling, will.'

Stendhal had accompanied Napoleon's armies around Europe, he had visited the ruins of Pompeii seven times and admired the Pont du Gard by a full moon at five in the morning ('The Coliseum in Rome hardly plunged me into a reverie more profound . . .').

Nietzsche's heroes had also fallen in love repeatedly. 'The whole movement of the world tends and leads towards copulation,' Montaigne had known. At the age of seventy-four, on holiday in Marienbad, Goethe had become infatuated with Ulrike von Levetzow, a pretty nineteen-year-old, whom he had invited out for tea and on walks, before asking for (and being refused) her hand in marriage. Stendhal, who had known and loved *Werther*, had been as passionate as its author, his diaries detailing conquests across decades. At twenty-four, stationed with the Napoleonic armies in Germany, he had taken the innkeeper's daughter to bed and noted proudly in his diary that she was 'the first German woman I ever saw who was totally exhausted after an orgasm. I made her passionate with my caresses; she was very frightened.'

And finally, these men had all been artists ('Art is the great stimulant to life,' recognized Nietzsche), and must have felt extraordinary satisfaction upon completing the *Essais, Il Socrate immaginario, Römische Elegien* and *De l'amour*.

8

These were, Nietzsche implied, some of the elements that human beings naturally needed for a fulfilled life. He added an important detail; that it was impossible to attain them without feeling very miserable some of the time:

> What if pleasure and displeasure were so tied together that whoever *wanted* to have as much as possible of one *must* also have as much as possible of the other . . . you have the choice: either *as little dis-*

pleasure as possible, painlessness in brief . . . or *as much displeasure as possible* as the price for the growth of an abundance of subtle pleasures and joys that have rarely been relished yet? If you decide for the former and desire to diminish and lower the level of human pain, you also have to diminish and lower the level of their *capacity for joy*.

The most fulfilling human projects appeared inseparable from a degree of torment, the sources of our greatest joys lying awkwardly close to those of our greatest pains:

Examine the lives of the best and most fruitful people and peoples and ask yourselves whether a tree that is supposed to grow to a proud height can dispense with bad weather and storms; whether misfortune and external resistance, some kinds of hatred, jealousy, stubbornness, mistrust, hardness, avarice, and violence do not belong among the *favourable* conditions without which any great growth even of virtue is scarcely possible.

9

Why? Because no one is able to produce a great work of art without experience, nor achieve a worldly position immediately, nor be a great lover at the first attempt; and in the interval between initial failure and subsequent success, in the gap between who we wish one day to be and who we are at present, must come pain, anxiety, envy and humiliation. We suffer because we cannot spontaneously master the ingredients of fulfilment.

Nietzsche was striving to correct the belief that fulfilment must come easily or not at all, a belief ruinous in its effects, for it leads us to withdraw prematurely from challenges that might have been overcome if only we had been prepared for the savagery legitimately demanded by almost everything valuable.

We might imagine that Montaigne's *Essays* had sprung fully formed from his mind and so could take the clumsiness of our own first attempts to write a philosophy of life as signs of a congenital incapacity for the task. We should look instead at the evidence of colossal authorial struggles behind the final masterpiece, the plethora of additions and revisions the *Essays* demanded.

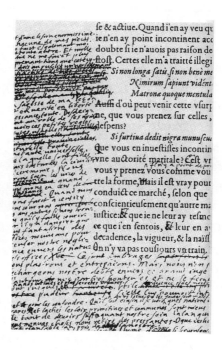

Le Rouge et le noir, Vie de Henry Brulard and *De l'amour* had been no easier to write. Stendhal had begun his artistic career by sketching out a number of poor plays. One had centred on the landing of an émigré army at Quiberon (the characters were to include William Pitt and Charles James Fox), another had charted Bonaparte's rise to power and a third – tentatively titled *L'Homme qui craint d'être gouverné* – had depicted the slide of an old man into senility. Stendhal had spent weeks at the Bibliothèque Nationale, copying out dictionary definitions of words like *'plaisanterie'*, *'ridicule'* and *'comique'* – but it had not been enough to transform his leaden playwriting. It was many decades of toil before the masterpieces emerged.

If most works of literature are less fine than *Le Rouge et le noir*, it is – suggested Nietzsche – not because their authors lack genius, but because they have an incorrect idea of how much pain is required. This is how hard one should try to write a novel:

> The recipe for becoming a good novelist . . . is easy to give, but to carry it out presupposes qualities one is accustomed to overlook when one says 'I do not have enough talent.' One has only to make a hundred or so sketches for novels, none longer than two pages but of such distinctness that every word in them is necessary; one should write down anecdotes every day until one has learnt how to give them the most pregnant and effective form; one should be tireless in collecting and describing human types and characters; one should above all relate things to others and listen to others relate, keeping one's eyes and ears open for the effect produced on those present, one should travel like a landscape painter or costume designer . . . one should, finally, reflect on the motives of human actions, disdain no signpost for instruction about them and be a collector of these things by day and night. One should continue in this many-sided exercise *for some ten years*; what is then created in the workshop . . . will be fit to go out into the world.

The philosophy amounted to a curious mixture of extreme faith in human potential (fulfilment is open to us all, as is the writing of great novels) and extreme toughness (we may need to spend a miserable decade on the first book).

It was in order to accustom us to the legitimacy of pain that Nietzsche spent so much time talking about mountains.

10

It is hard to read more than a few pages without coming upon an alpine reference:

> **Ecce Homo:** He who knows how to breathe the air of my writings knows that it is an air of heights, a *robust* air. One has to be made for it, otherwise there is no small danger one will catch cold. The ice is near, the solitude is terrible – but how peacefully all things lie in the light! how freely one breathes! how much one feels *beneath* one!

Philosophy, as I have hitherto understood and lived it, is a voluntary living in ice and high mountains.

On the Genealogy of Morals: We would need *another* sort of spirit than those we are likely to encounter in this age [to understand my philosophy] . . . they would need to be acclimatized to thinner air higher up, to winter treks, ice and mountains in every sense.

Human, All Too Human: In the mountains of truth you will never climb in vain: either you will get up higher today or you will exercise your strength so as to be able to get up higher tomorrow.

Untimely Meditations: To climb as high into the pure icy Alpine air as a philosopher ever climbed, up to where all the mist and obscurity cease and where the fundamental constitution of things speaks in voice rough and rigid but ineluctably comprehensible!

He was – in both a practical and spiritual sense – of the mountains. Having taken citizenship in April 1869, Nietzsche may be considered Switzerland's most famous philosopher. Even so, he on occasion succumbed to a sentiment with which few Swiss are unacquainted. 'I am distressed to be Swiss!' he complained to his mother a year after taking up citizenship.

Upon resigning his post at Basle University at the age of thirty-five, he began spending winters by the Mediterranean, largely in Genoa and Nice, and summers in the Alps, in the small village of Sils-Maria, 1,800 metres above sea-level in the Engadine region of south-eastern Switzerland, a few kilometres from St Moritz, where the winds from Italy collide with cooler northern gusts and turn the sky an aquamarine blue.

Nietzsche visited the Engadine for the first time in June 1879 and at once fell in love with the climate and topography. 'I now have Europe's best and mightiest air to breathe,' he told Paul Rée, 'its nature is akin to my own.' To Peter Gast, he wrote, 'This is not Switzerland . . . but something quite different, at least much more southern – I would have to go to the high plateaux of Mexico overlooking the Pacific to find anything similar (for example, Oaxaca), and the vegetation there would of course be tropical. Well, I shall try to keep this Sils-Maria for myself.' And to his old schoolfriend

Carl von Gersdorff, he explained, 'I feel that here and nowhere else is my real home and breeding ground.'

Nietzsche spent seven summers in Sils-Maria in a rented room in a chalet with views on to pine trees and mountains. There he wrote all or substantial portions of *The Gay Science, Thus Spake Zarathustra, Beyond Good and Evil, On the Genealogy of Morals* and *Twilight of the Idols*. He would rise at five in the morning and work until midday, then take walks up the huge peaks that necklace the village, Piz Corvatsch, Piz Lagrev, Piz de la Margna, jagged and raw mountains that look as if they had only recently thrust through the earth's crust under atrocious tectonic pressures. In the evening, alone in his room, he would eat a few slices of ham, an egg and a roll and go to bed early. ('How can anyone become a thinker if he does not spend at least a third of the day without passions, people and books?')

Today, inevitably, there is a museum in the village. For a few francs, one is invited to visit the philosopher's bedroom, refurbished, the guidebook explains, 'as it looked in Nietzsche's time, in all its unpretentiousness'.

Yet to understand why Nietzsche felt there to be such an affinity between his philosophy and the mountains, it may be best to skirt the room and visit instead one of Sils-Maria's many sports shops in order to acquire walking boots, a rucksack, a water-bottle, gloves, a compass and a pick.

A hike up Piz Corvatsch, a few kilometres from Nietzsche's house, will explain better than any museum the spirit of his philosophy, his defence of difficulty, and his reasons for turning away from Schopenhauerian deer-like shyness.

At the base of the mountain one finds a large car park, a row of recycling bins, a depot for rubbish trucks and a restaurant offering oleaginous sausages and rösti.

The summit is, by contrast, sublime. There are views across the entire Engadine: the turquoise lakes of Segl, Silvaplana and St Moritz, and to the south, near the border with Italy, the massive Sella and Roseg glaciers. There is an extraordinary stillness in the air, it seems one can touch the roof of the world. The height leaves one out of breath but curiously elated. It is hard not to start grinning, perhaps laughing, for no particular reason, an innocent laughter that comes from the core of one's being and expresses a primal delight at being alive to see such beauty.

But, to come to the moral of Nietzsche's mountain philosophy, it isn't easy to climb 3,451 metres above sea-level. It requires five hours at least, one must cling to steep paths, negotiate a way around boulders and through thick pine-forests, grow breathless in the thin air, add layers of clothes to fight the wind and crunch through eternal snows.

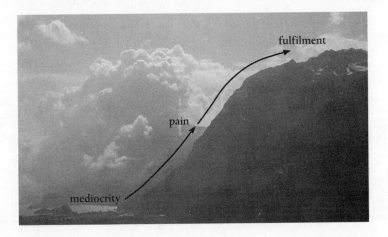

11

Nietzsche offered another alpine metaphor. A few steps from his room in Sils-Maria a path leads to the Fex Valley, one of the most fertile of the Engadine. Its gentle slopes are extensively farmed. In summer, families of cows stand reflectively munching the almost luminously rich-green grass, their bells clanging as they move from one patch to another.

Streams trickle through the fields with the sound of sparkling water being poured into glasses. Beside many small, immaculate farms (each one flying the national and cantonal flags) stand carefully tended vegetable gardens from whose loamy soils sprout vigorous cauliflowers, beetroots, carrots and lettuces, which tempt one to kneel down and take rabbit-like bites out of them.

If there are such nice lettuces here, it is because the Fex Valley is glacial, with the characteristic mineral richness of soil once a glacial mantle has retreated. Much further along the valley, hours of strenuous walking from the tidy farms, one comes upon the glacier itself, massive and terrifying. It looks like a tablecloth waiting for a tug to straighten out its folds, but these folds are the size of houses and are made of razor-sharp ice, and occasionally release agonized bellows as they rearrange themselves in the summer sun.

It is hard to conceive, when standing at the edge of the cruel glacier, how this frozen bulk could have a role to play in the gestation of vegetables and lush grass only a few kilometres along the valley, to imagine that something as apparently antithetical to a green field as a glacier could be responsible for the field's fertility.

Nietzsche, who often walked in the Fex Valley carrying a pencil and leather-bound notebook ('Only thoughts which come from *walking* have any value'), drew an analogy with the dependence of positive elements in human life on negative ones, of fulfilment on difficulties:

> When we behold those deeply-furrowed hollows in which glaciers have lain, we think it hardly possible that a time will come when a wooded, grassy valley, watered by streams, will spread itself out upon the same spot. So it is, too, in the history of mankind: the most savage forces beat a path, and are mainly destructive; but their work was none-the-less necessary, in order that later a gentler civilization might raise its house. The frightful energies – those which are called evil – are the cyclopean architects and road-makers of humanity.

12

But frightful difficulties are sadly, of course, not enough. All lives are difficult; what makes some of them fulfilled as well is the manner in which pains have been met. Every pain is an indistinct signal that something is wrong, which may engender either a good or bad result depending on the sagacity and strength of mind of the sufferer. Anxiety may precipitate panic, or an accurate analysis of what is amiss. A sense of injustice may lead to murder, or to a ground-breaking work of economic theory. Envy may lead to bitterness, or to a decision to compete with a rival and the production of a masterpiece.

As Nietzsche's beloved Montaigne had explained in the final chapter of the *Essays*, the art of living lies in finding uses for our adversities:

We must learn to suffer whatever we cannot avoid. Our life is composed, like the harmony of the world, of discords as well as of different tones, sweet and harsh, sharp and flat, soft and loud. If a musician liked only some of them, what could he sing? He has got to know how to use all of them and blend them together. So too must we with good and ill, which are of one substance with our life.

And some 300 years later, Nietzsche returned to the thought:

If only we were fruitful fields, we would at bottom let nothing perish unused and see in every event, thing and man welcome manure.

How then to be fruitful?

13

Born in Urbino in 1483, Raphael from an early age displayed such an interest in drawing that his father took the boy to Perugia to work as an apprentice to the renowned Pietro Perugino. He was soon executing works of his own and by his late teens had painted several portraits of members of the court of Urbino, and altarpieces for churches in Città di Castello, a day's ride from Urbino across the mountains on the road to Perugia.

But Raphael, one of Nietzsche's favourite painters, knew he was not then a great artist, for he had seen the works of two men, Michelangelo Buonarroti and Leonardo da Vinci. They had shown him that he was unable to paint figures in motion, and despite an aptitude for pictorial geometry, that he had no grasp of linear perspective. The envy could have grown monstrous. Raphael turned it into manure instead.

In 1504, at the age of twenty-one, he left Urbino for Florence in order to study the work of his two masters. He examined their cartoons in the Hall of the Great Council where Leonardo had worked on the Battle of Anghiari and Michelangelo on the Battle of Cascina. He imbibed the lessons of Leonardo and Michelangelo's anatomical drawings and followed their example of dissecting and drawing corpses. He learned from Leonardo's *Adoration of the Magi* and his cartoons of the Virgin and Child, and looked closely at an unusual portrait Leonardo had been asked to execute for a nobleman, Francesco del Giocondo, who had wanted a likeness of his wife, a young beauty with a somewhat enigmatic smile.

The results of Raphael's exertions were soon apparent. We can compare *Portrait of a Young Woman* which Raphael had drawn before moving to Florence with *Portrait of a Woman* completed a few years after.

Mona had given Raphael the idea of a half-length seated pose in which the arms provided the base of a pyramidal composition. She had taught him how to use contrasting axes for the head, shoulder and hands in order to lend volume to a figure. Whereas the woman drawn in Urbino had looked awkwardly constricted in her clothes, her arms unnaturally cut off, the woman from Florence was mobile and at ease.

Raphael had not spontaneously come into possession of his talents; he had become great by responding intelligently to a sense of inferiority that would have led lesser men to despair.

The career path offered a Nietzschean lesson in the benefits of wisely interpreted pain:

> Don't talk about giftedness, inborn talents! One can name all kinds of great men who were not very gifted. They *acquired* greatness, became 'geniuses' (as we put it) through qualities about whose lack no man aware of them likes to speak: all of them had that diligent seriousness of a craftsman, learning first to construct the parts properly before daring to make a great whole. They allowed themselves time for it, because they took more pleasure in making the little, secondary things well than in the effect of a dazzling whole.

Raphael: studies for Niccolini-Cowper Madonna;
Niccolini-Cowper Madonna

Raphael had been able – to use Nietzsche's terms – to sublimate (*sublimieren*), spiritualize (*vergeistigen*) and raise (*aufheben*) to fruitfulness the difficulties in his path.

14

The philosopher had a practical as well as a metaphorical interest in horticulture. On resigning from Basle University in 1879, Nietzsche had set his heart on becoming a professional gardener. 'You know that my preference is for a simple, natural way of life,' he informed his surprised mother, 'and I am becoming increasingly eager for it. There is no other cure for my health. I need real *work*, which takes time and induces *tiredness* without mental strain.' He remembered an old tower in Naumburg near his mother's house, which he planned to rent while looking after the adjoining garden. The gardening life began with enthusiasm in September 1879 – but there were soon problems. Nietzsche's poor eyesight prevented him from seeing what he was trimming, he had difficulty bending his back, there were too many leaves (it was autumn) and after three weeks, he felt he had no alternative but to give up.

Yet traces of his horticultural enthusiasm survived in his philosophy, for in certain passages, he proposed that we should look at our difficulties like gardeners. At their roots, plants can be odd and unpleasant, but a person with knowledge and faith in their potential will lead them to bear beautiful flowers and fruit – just as, in life, at root level, there may be difficult emotions and situations which can nevertheless result, through careful cultivation, in the greatest achievements and joys.

One can dispose of one's drives like a gardener and, though few know it, cultivate the shoots of anger, pity, curiosity, vanity as productively and profitably as a beautiful fruit tree on a trellis.

Art, beauty, love

Anger, pity,
curiousity, vanity

But most of us fail to recognize the debt we owe to these shoots of
difficulty. We are liable to think that anxiety and envy have nothing legitimate to teach us and so remove them like emotional
weeds. We believe, as Nietzsche put it, that 'the higher *is not
allowed* to grow out of the lower, *is not allowed* to have grown at
all . . . everything first-rate must be *causa sui* [the cause of itself].'

Yet 'good and honoured things' were, Nietzsche stressed, 'art-
fully related, knotted and crocheted to . . . wicked, apparently antithetical things'. 'Love and hate, gratitude and revenge, good nature
and anger . . . belong together,' which does not mean that they
have to be *expressed* together, but that a positive may be the result
of a negative successfully gardened. Therefore:

> The emotions of hatred, envy, covetousness and lust for domina-
> tion [are] life-conditioning emotions . . . which must fundamentally
> and essentially be present in the total economy of life.

To cut out every negative root would simultaneously mean chok-
ing off positive elements that might arise from it further up the
stem of the plant.

We should not feel embarrassed by our difficulties, only by our
failure to grow anything beautiful from them.

15

It was for their apparent appreciation of the point that Nietzsche looked back in admiration to the ancient Greeks.

It is tempting when contemplating their serene temples at dusk, like those at Paestum, a few kilometres from Sorrento – which Nietzsche visited with Malwida von Meysenbug in early 1877 – to imagine that the Greeks were an unusually measured people whose temples were the outward manifestations of an order they felt within themselves and their society.

This had been the opinion of the great classicist Johann Winckelmann (1717–68) and had won over successive generations of German university professors. But Nietzsche proposed that far from arising out of serenity, classical Greek civilization had arisen from the sublimation of the most sinister forces:

> The greater and more terrible the passions are that an age, a people,
> an individual can permit themselves, because they are capable of
> employing them as *a means, the higher stands their culture.*

The temples might have looked calm, but they were the flowers of well-gardened plants with dark roots. The Dionysiac festivals showed both the darkness and the attempt to control and cultivate it:

> Nothing astonishes the observer of the Greek world more than when
> he discovers that from time to time the Greeks made as it were a
> festival of all their passions and evil natural inclinations and even

instituted a kind of official order of proceedings in the celebration of what was all-too-human in them . . . They took this all-too-human to be inescapable and, instead of reviling it, preferred to accord it a kind of right of the second rank through regulating it within the usages of society and religion: indeed, everything in man possessing *power* they called divine and inscribed it on the walls of their Heaven. They do not repudiate the natural drive that finds expression in the evil qualities but regulate it and, as soon as they have discovered sufficient prescriptive measures to provide these wild waters with the least harmful means of channeling and outflow, confine them to definite cults and days. This is the root of all the moral free-mindedness of antiquity. One granted to the evil and suspicious . . . a moderate discharge, and did not strive after their total annihilation.

The Greeks did not cut out their adversities; they cultivated them:

All passions have a phase when they are merely disastrous, in which they draw their victims down by weight of stupidity – and a later, very much later one in which they marry the spirit, 'spiritualize' themselves. In former times, because of the stupidity of passion, people waged war on passion itself: they plotted to destroy it . . . *Destroying* the passions and desires merely in order to avoid their stupidity and the disagreeable consequences of their stupidity seems to us nowadays to be itself simply an acute form of stupidity. We no longer marvel at dentists who *pull out* teeth to stop them hurting.

Fulfilment is reached by responding wisely to difficulties that could tear one apart. Squeamish spirits may be tempted to pull the molar out at once or come off Piz Corvatsch on the lower slopes. Nietzsche urged us to endure.

16

And far from coincidentally, never to drink.

> *Dear Mother,*
> *If I write to you today, it is about one of the most unpleasant and painful*
> *incidents I have ever been responsible for. In fact, I have misbehaved very*
> *badly, and I don't know whether you can or will forgive me. I pick up my*
> *pen most reluctantly and with a heavy heart, especially when I think back*
> *to our pleasant life together during the Easter holidays, which was never*
> *spoiled by any discord. Last Sunday, I got drunk, and I have no excuse,*
> *except that I did not know how much I could take, and I was rather*
> *excited in the afternoon.*

So wrote eighteen-year-old Friedrich to his mother Franziska after four glasses of beer in the halls of Attenburg near his school in the spring of 1863. A few years later, at Bonn and Leipzig universities, he felt irritation with his fellow students for their love of alcohol: 'I often found the expressions of good fellowship in the clubhouse extremely distasteful ... I could hardly bear certain individuals because of their beery materialism.'

Nietzsche's student fraternity at Bonn University.
Nietzsche is in the second row, leaning to one side.
Note, in the row below, the fraternity beerkeg.

The attitude remained constant throughout the philosopher's adult life:

> Alcoholic drinks are no good for me; a glass of wine or beer a day is quite enough to make life for me a 'Vale of Tears' – Munich is where my antipodes live.

'How much *beer* there is in the German intelligence!' he complained. 'Perhaps the modern European discontent is due to the fact that our forefathers were given to drinking through the entire Middle Ages . . . The Middle Ages meant the alcohol poisoning of Europe.'

In the spring of 1871, Nietzsche went on holiday with his sister to the Hôtel du Parc in Lugano. The hotel bill for 2–9 March shows that he drank fourteen glasses of milk.

It was more than a personal taste. Anyone seeking to be happy was strongly advised never to drink anything alcoholic at all. Never:

> I cannot advise all *more spiritual* natures too seriously to abstain from alcohol absolutely. *Water* suffices.

Why? Because Raphael had not drunk to escape his envy in Urbino in 1504, he had gone to Florence and learned how to be a great painter. Because Stendhal had not drunk in 1805 to escape his despair over *L'Homme qui craint d'être gouverné*, he had gardened the pain for seventeen years and published *De l'amour* in 1822:

> If you refuse to let your own suffering lie upon you even for an hour and if you constantly try to prevent and forestall all possible distress way ahead of time; if you experience suffering and

displeasure as evil, hateful, worthy of annihilation, and as a defect of existence, then it is clear that [you harbour in your heart] . . . the *religion of comfortableness*. How little you know of human *happiness*, you comfortable . . . people, for happiness and unhappiness are sisters and even twins that either grow up together or, as in your case, *remain small* together.

17

Nietzsche's antipathy to alcohol explains simultaneously his antipathy to what had been the dominant British school of moral philosophy: Utilitarianism, and its greatest proponent, John Stuart Mill. The Utilitarians had argued that in a world beset by moral ambiguities, the way to judge whether an action was right or wrong was to measure the amount of pleasure and pain it gave rise to. Mill proposed that:

[A]ctions are right in proportion as they tend to promote happiness, wrong as they tend to produce the reverse of happiness. By happiness is intended pleasure, and the absence of pain; by unhappiness, pain, and the privation of pleasure.

The thought of Utilitarianism, and even the nation from which it had sprung, enraged Nietzsche:

European vulgarity, the plebeianism of modern ideas [is the work and invention of] *England*.

Man does *not* strive for happiness; only the English do that.

He was, of course, also striving for happiness; he simply believed that it could not be attained as painlessly as the Utilitarians appeared to be suggesting:

All these modes of thought which assess the value of things according to *pleasure* and *pain*, that is to say according to attendant and secondary phenomena, are foreground modes of thought and naïveties which anyone conscious of *creative* powers and an artist's conscience will look down on with derision.

An artist's conscience because artistic creation offers a most explicit example of an activity which may deliver immense fulfilment but always demands immense suffering. Had Stendhal assessed the value of his art according to the 'pleasure' and 'pain' it had at once brought him, there would have been no advance from *L'Homme qui craint d'être gouverné* to the summit of his powers.

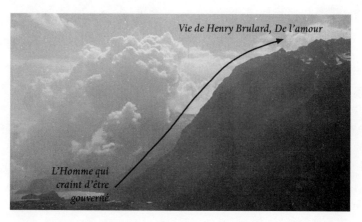

Instead of drinking beer in the lowlands, Nietzsche asked us to accept the pain of the climb. He also offered a suggestion for town-planners:

> The secret for harvesting from existence the greatest fruitfulness and the greatest enjoyment is – to *live dangerously*! Build your cities on the slopes of Vesuvius!

Vesuvius, exploding in 1879, three years before
the above statement was written

And if one were still tempted to have a drink, but had no high opinion of Christianity, Nietzsche added a further argument to dissuade one from doing so. Anyone who liked drinking had, he argued, a fundamentally Christian outlook on life:

> To believe that wine *makes cheerful* I would have to be a Christian,
> that is to say believe what is for me in particular an absurdity.

18

He had more experience of Christianity than of alcohol. He was born in the tiny village of Röcken near Leipzig in Saxony. His father, Carl Ludwig Nietzsche, was the parson, his deeply devout mother was herself the daughter of a parson, David Ernst Oehler, who took services in the village of Pobles an hour away. Their son was baptized before an assembly of the local clergy in Röcken church in October 1844.

Friedrich loved his father, who died when he was only four, and revered his memory throughout his life. On the one occasion when he had a little money, after winning a court case against a publisher in 1885, he ordered a large headstone for his father's grave on which he had carved a quotation from Corinthians (1 Cor 13.8):

> *Die Liebe höret nimmer auf*
> Charity never faileth

'He was the perfect embodiment of a country pastor,' Nietzsche recalled of Carl Ludwig. 'A tall, delicate figure, a fine-featured face, amiable and beneficent. Everywhere welcomed and beloved as much for his witty conversation as for his warm sympathy, esteemed and loved by the farmers, extending blessings by word and deed in his capacity as a spiritual guide.'

Yet this filial love did not prevent Nietzsche from harbouring the deepest reservations about the consolation that his father, and Christianity in general, could offer those in pain:

> I bring against the Christian Church the most terrible charge any prosecutor has ever uttered. To me it is the extremest thinkable form of corruption ... [it] has left nothing untouched by its depravity ... I call Christianity the *one* great curse, the *one* great intrinsic depravity ...
>
> One does well to put gloves on when reading the New Testament. The proximity of so much uncleanliness almost forces one to do so ... Everything in it is cowardice, everything is self-deception and closing one's eyes to oneself ... Do I still have to add that in the entire New Testament there is only *one* solitary figure one is obliged to respect? Pilate, the Roman governor.

Quite simply:

> It is indecent to be a Christian today.

19

How does the New Testament console us for our difficulties? By suggesting that many of these are not difficulties at all but rather virtues:

If one is worried about timidity, the New Testament points out:
Blessed are the meek: for they shall inherit the earth. (Matthew 5.5)
If one is worried about having no friends, the New Testament suggests:
Blessed are ye, when men shall hate you, and when they shall separate you from their company, and shall reproach you, and cast out your name as evil . . . your reward is great in heaven. (Luke 6.22–3)
If one is worried about an exploitative job, the New Testament advises:
Servants, obey in all things your masters according to the flesh . . . Knowing that of the Lord ye shall receive the reward of the inheritance: for ye serve the Lord Christ. (Colossians 3.22–4)
If one is worried at having no money, the New Testament tells us:
It is easier for a camel to go through the eye of a needle, than for a rich man to enter into the kingdom of God. (Mark 10.25)

There may be differences between such words and a drink but Nietzsche insisted on an essential equivalence. Both Christianity and alcohol have the power to convince us that what we previously thought deficient in ourselves and the world does not require attention; both weaken our resolve to garden our problems; both deny us the chance of fulfilment:

The two great European narcotics, alcohol and Christianity.

Christianity had, in Nietzsche's account, emerged from the minds of timid slaves in the Roman Empire who had lacked the stomach to climb to the tops of mountains, and so had built themselves a philosophy claiming that their bases were delightful. Christians had wished to enjoy the real ingredients of fulfilment (a position in the world, sex, intellectual mastery, creativity) but did not have the courage to endure the difficulties these goods demanded. They had therefore fashioned a hypocritical creed denouncing what they wanted but were too weak to fight for while praising what they did not want but happened to have. Powerlessness became 'goodness', baseness 'humility', submission to people one hated 'obedience' and, in Nietzsche's phrase, 'not-being-able-to-take-revenge' turned into 'forgiveness'. Every feeling of weakness was overlaid with a sanctifying name, and made to seem 'a voluntary achievement, something wanted, chosen, a *deed*, an *accomplishment*'. Addicted to 'the religion of comfortableness', Christians, in their value system, had given precedence to what was easy, not what was desirable, and so had drained life of its potential.

20

Having a 'Christian' perspective on difficulty is not limited to members of the Christian church; it is for Nietzsche a permanent psychological possibility. We all become Christians when we profess indifference to what we secretly long for but do not have; when we blithely say that we do not need love or a position in the world, money or success, creativity or health – while the corners of our mouths twitch with bitterness; and we wage silent wars against what we have publicly renounced, firing shots over the parapet, sniping from the trees.

How would Nietzsche have preferred us to approach our setbacks? To continue to believe in what we wish for, *even when we do not have it, and may never.* Put another way, to resist the temptation to denigrate and declare evil certain goods because they have proved hard to secure – a pattern of behaviour of which Nietzsche's own, infinitely tragic life offers us perhaps the best model.

21

Epicurus had from an early age been among his favourite ancient philosophers; he called him 'the soul-soother of later antiquity', 'one of the greatest men, the inventor of an heroic-idyllic mode of philosophizing'. What especially appealed to him was Epicurus's idea that happiness involved a life among friends. But he was rarely to know the contentment of community: 'It is our lot to be intellectual hermits and occasionally to have a conversation with someone like-minded.' At thirty, he composed a hymn to loneliness, *'Hymnus auf die Einsamkeit'*, which he did not have the heart to finish.

The search for a wife was no less sorrowful, the problem partly caused by Nietzsche's appearance – his extraordinarily large walrus moustache – and his shyness, which bred the gauche stiff manner of a retired colonel. In the spring of 1876, on a trip to Geneva, Nietzsche fell in love with a twenty-three-year-old, green-eyed blonde, Mathilde Trampedach. During a conversation on the poetry of Henry Longfellow, Nietzsche mentioned that he had never come across a German version of Longfellow's 'Excelsior'. Mathilde said she had one at home and offered to copy it out for him. Encouraged, Nietzsche invited her out for a walk. She brought her landlady as a chaperone. A few days later, he offered to play the piano for her, and the next she heard from the thirty-one-year-old Professor of Classical Philology at Basle University was a request for marriage. 'Do you not think that together each of us will be better and more free than either of us could be alone – and so *excelsior*?' asked the playful colonel. 'Will you dare to come with me . . . on all the paths of living and thinking?' Mathilde didn't dare.

A succession of similar rejections took their toll. In the light of his depression and ill health, Richard Wagner decided that there were two possible remedies: 'He must either marry or write an opera.' But Nietzsche couldn't write an opera, and apparently lacked the talent to produce even a decent tune. (In July 1872, he sent the conductor Hans von Bülow a piano duet he had written, asking for an honest appraisal. It was, replied von Bülow, 'the most extreme fantastical extravagance, the most irritating and anti-musical set of notes on manuscript paper I have seen for a long time', and he wondered whether Nietzsche might have been pulling his leg. 'You designated your music as "frightful" – it truly is.')

Wagner grew more insistent. 'For Heaven's sake, marry a rich woman!' he intoned, and entered into communication with Nietzsche's doctor, Otto Eiser, with whom he speculated that the philosopher's ill health was caused by excessive masturbation. It was an irony lost on Wagner that the one rich woman with whom Nietzsche was truly in love was Wagner's own wife, Cosima. For years, he carefully disguised his feelings for her under the cloak of friendly solicitude. It was only once he had lost his reason that the reality emerged. 'Ariadne, I love you,' wrote Nietzsche, or, as he signed himself, Dionysus, in a postcard sent to Cosima from Turin at the beginning of January 1889.

Nevertheless, Nietzsche intermittently agreed with the Wagnerian thesis on the importance of marriage. In a letter to his married friend Franz Overbeck, he complained, 'Thanks to your wife, things are a hundred times better for you than for me. You have a nest together. I have, at best, a *cave* . . . Occasional contact with people is like a holiday, a redemption from "me".'

In 1882, he hoped once more that he had found a suitable wife, Lou Andreas-Salomé, his greatest, most painful love. She was twenty-one, beautiful, clever, flirtatious and fascinated by his philosophy. Nietzsche was defenceless. 'I want to be lonely no longer, but to learn again to be a human being. Ah, here I have practically everything to learn!' he told her. They spent two weeks together in the Tautenburg forest and in Lucerne posed with their mutual friend Paul Rée for an unusual photograph.

But Lou was more interested in Nietzsche as a philosopher than as a husband. The rejection threw him into renewed prolonged, violent depression. 'My lack of confidence is now immense,' he told Overbeck, 'everything I hear makes me think that people despise me.' He felt particular bitterness towards his mother and sister, who had meddled in the relationship with Lou, and now broke off contact with them, deepening his isolation. ('I do not like my mother, and it is painful for me to hear my sister's voice. I always became ill when I was with them.')

There were professional difficulties, too. None of his books sold more than 2,000 copies in his sane life-time; most sold a few hundred. With only a modest pension and some shares inherited from an aunt on which to survive, the author could rarely pay for new clothes, and ended up looking, in his words, 'scraped like a mountain sheep'. In hotels, he stayed in the cheapest rooms, often fell into arrears with the rent and could afford neither heating nor the hams and sausages he loved.

His health was as problematic. From his schooldays, he had suffered from a range of ailments: headaches, indigestion, vomiting, dizziness, near blindness and insomnia, many of these the symptoms of the syphilis he had almost certainly contracted in a Cologne brothel in February 1865 (though Nietzsche claimed he had come away without touching anything except a piano). In a letter to Malwida von Meysenbug written three years after his trip to Sorrento, he explained, 'As regards torment and self-denial, my life during these past years can match that of any ascetic of any time . . .' And to his doctor he reported, 'Constant pain, a feeling of being half-paralysed, a condition closely related to seasickness, during which I find it difficult to speak – this feeling lasts several hours a day. For my diversion I have raging seizures (the most recent one forced me to vomit for three days and three nights; I thirsted after death). Can't read! Only seldom can I write! Can't deal with my fellows! Can't listen to music!'

Finally, at the beginning of January 1889, Nietzsche broke down in Turin's Piazza Carlo Alberto and embraced a horse, was carried back to his boarding-house, where he thought of shooting the Kaiser, planned a war against anti-Semites, and grew certain that he was – depending on the hour – Dionysus, Jesus, God, Napoleon, the King of Italy, Buddha, Alexander the Great, Caesar, Voltaire, Alexander Herzen and Richard Wagner; before he was bundled into a train and taken to an asylum in Germany to be looked after by his elderly mother and sister until his death eleven years later at the age of fifty-five.

22

And yet through appalling loneliness, obscurity, poverty and ill health, Nietzsche did not manifest the behaviour of which he had accused Christians; he did not take against friendship, he did not attack eminence, wealth, or well-being. The Abbé Galiani and Goethe remained heroes. Though Mathilde had wished for no more than a conversation about poetry, he continued to believe that 'for the male sickness of self-contempt the surest cure is to be loved by a clever woman.' Though sickly and lacking Montaigne or Stendhal's dexterity on a horse, he remained attached to the idea of an active life: 'Early in the morning, at break of day, in all the freshness and dawn of one's strength, to read a *book* – I call that vicious!'

He fought hard to be happy, but where he did not succeed he did not turn against what he had once aspired to. He remained committed to what was in his eyes the most important characteristic of a noble human being: to be someone who *'no longer denies'*.

23

After seven hours of walking, much of it in the rain, it was in a state of extreme exhaustion that I reached the summit of Piz Corvatsch, high above the clouds that decked the Engadine valleys below. In my rucksack I carried a water-bottle, an Emmental sandwich and an envelope from the Hotel Edelweiss in Sils-Maria on which I had that morning written a quote from the mountain philosopher, with the intention of facing Italy and reading it to the wind and the rocks at 3,400 metres.

Like his pastor father, Nietzsche had been committed to the task of consolation. Like his father, he had wished to offer us paths to fulfilment. But unlike pastors, and dentists who pull out throbbing teeth and gardeners who destroy plants with ill-favoured roots, he had judged difficulties to be a critical prerequisite of fulfilment, and hence knew saccharine consolations to be ultimately more cruel than helpful:

The worst sickness of men has originated in the way they have combated their sicknesses. What seemed a cure has in the long run produced something worse than what it was supposed to overcome. The means which worked immediately, anaesthetizing and intoxicating, *the so-called consolations*, were ignorantly supposed to

be actual cures. The fact was not noticed ... that these instant-
aneous alleviations often had to be paid for with a general and
profound worsening of the complaint.

Not everything which makes us feel better is good for us. Not
everything which hurts may be bad.

*To regard states of distress in general as an objection, as something that
must be abolished, is the [supreme idiocy], in a general sense a real disaster
in its consequences . . . almost as stupid as the will to abolish bad weather.*

Notes

Acknowledgements

Copyright Acknowledgements

Picture Acknowledgements

Index

Notes

Consolation for Unpopularity

Aside from a mention of Aristophanes and quotations from Plato's *Phaedo*, the portrait of Socrates is drawn from Plato's early and middle dialogues (the so-called Socratic dialogues): *Apology, Charmides, Crito, Euthydemus, Euthyphro, Gorgias, Hippias Major, Hippias Minor, Ion, Laches, Lysis, Menexenus, Meno, Protagoras* and *Republic*, book I.

Quotations taken from:
The Last Days of Socrates, Plato, translated by Hugh Tredennick, Penguin, 1987
Early Socratic Dialogues, Plato, translated by Iain Lane, Penguin, 1987
Protagoras and Meno, Plato, translated by W. K. C. Guthrie, Penguin, 1987
Gorgias, Plato, translated by Robin Waterfield, OUP, 1994.

p. 4 So . . . deaths: *Apology*, 29d
p. 15 Whenever . . . angle: *Laches*, 188a
p. 18 Let's . . . courageous: *Laches*, 190e–191a
p. 18 At . . . battle: *Laches*, 191c
p. 20 By . . . inescapable: *Meno*, 78c–79a
p. 28 I . . . cities: *Apology*, 36b
p. 28 I . . . well-being: *Apology*, 36d
pp. 28–9 I . . . fellow-citizen: *Apology*, 29d
p. 29 I . . . narrow: *Apology*, 36a
p. 32 If . . . choose: *Gorgias*, 472a–b
pp. 32–3 The . . . him: *Gorgias*, 471e–472a
p. 34 When . . . public: *Crito*, 47b
p. 34 Don't . . . say: *Crito*, 47a–48a
p. 36 I . . . time: *Apology*, 37a–b
p. 37 If . . . sleeping: *Apology*, 30d–31a
p. 39 In . . . off: *Phaedo*, 116c–d
p. 39 When . . . himself: *Phaedo*, 117a–d
p. 40 What . . . friends!: *Phaedo*, 117d
p. 40 And . . . man: *Phaedo*, 118a

Consolation for Not Having Enough Money

Quotations taken from:
The Essential Epicurus, Epicurus, translated by Eugene O'Connor, Prometheus Books, 1993
The Epicurean Inscription, Diogenes of Oinoanda, translated by Martin Ferguson Smith, Bibliopolis, 1993
On the Nature of the Universe, Lucretius, translated by R. E. Latham, revised by John Godwin, Penguin, 1994

p. 50 If . . . forms: *Fragments*, VI.10
p. 50 Pleasure . . . life: *Letter to Menoeceus*, 128
p. 50 The . . . this: *Fragments*, 59
pp. 50–51 The . . . happiness: *Letter to Menoeceus*, 122
p. 55 A . . . malady: Lucretius, *De Rerum Natura*, III.1070
p. 55 Just . . . mind: *Fragments*, 54
p. 56 Send . . . like: *Fragments*, 39
p. 57 Of . . . friendship: *Principal Doctrines*, 27
p. 57 Before . . . wolf: quoted in Seneca, *Epistle*, XIX.10
p. 58 We . . . politics: *Vatican Sayings*, 58
p. 58 The . . . pleasant: *Letter to Menoeceus*, 126
p. 59 What . . . anticipation: *Letter to Menoeceus*, 124–5
p. 59 There . . . living: *Letter to Menoeceus*, 125

p. 60 Of . . . necessary: *Principal Doctrines*, 29

p. 61 Plain . . . away: *Letter to Menoeceus*, 130

p. 62 As . . . without: Porphyry reporting Epicurus's view in *On Abstinence*, 1.51.6–52.1

p. 62 Nothing . . . little: *Fragments*, 69

p. 63 The . . . accomplished?: *Vatican Sayings*, 71

p. 64 The . . . joy: *Vatican Sayings*, 81

p. 65 idle opinions: *Principal Doctrines*, 29

p. 67 Luxurious . . . flesh: Diogenes of Oinoanda, Fragment 109

p. 67 One . . . overflowing: Diogenes of Oinoanda, Fragment 108

p. 67 Real . . . science: Diogenes of Oinoanda, Fragment 2

p. 67 Having . . . salvation: Diogenes of Oinoanda, Fragment 3 (adapted)

p. 68 chosen . . . senses: Lucretius, *De Rerum Natura*, v.1133–4

p. 68 send . . . like: Fragments, 39

p. 69 ergo . . . *herbas*: Lucretius, *De Rerum Natura*, 11.20–33

p. 70 When . . . poverty: *Vatican Sayings*, 25

p. 70 Mankind . . . seas: Lucretius, *De Rerum Natura*, v.1430–5

p. 70 It . . . good: *Letter to Menoeceus*, 129

Consolation for Frustration

Quotations taken from:

The Annals of Imperial Rome, Tacitus, translated by Michael Grant, Penguin, 1996

The Twelve Caesars, Suetonius, translated by Robert Graves, Penguin, 1991

Dialogues and Letters, Seneca, translated by C. D. N. Costa, Penguin, 1997

Letters from a Stoic, Seneca, translated by Robin Campbell, Penguin, 1969

Moral Essays, volume i, Seneca, translated by John W. Basore, Loeb-Harvard, 1994

Moral Essays, volume ii, Seneca, translated by John W. Basore, Loeb-Harvard, 1996

Moral and Political Essays, Seneca,

translated by John M. Cooper and J. F. Procopé, CUP, 1995

Naturales Quaestiones i & ii, Seneca, translated by T. H. Corcoran, Loeb-Harvard, 1972

p. 76 Where . . . tutor: *Tacitus*, xv.62

p. 76 I . . . end: *Tacitus*, xv.63

p. 77 He . . . undisturbed: *Epistulae Morales*, civ.28–9

p. 78 the Monster: Suetonius, *Caligula*, iv.22

p. 78 on . . . neck!: Suetonius, *Caligula*, iv.30

p. 79 I . . . it: *Epistulae Morales*, lxxviii.3

p. 82 There . . . vices: *De Ira*, 11.36.5–6

p. 84 Prosperity . . . tempers: *De Ira*, 11.21.7

p. 84 What . . . columns?: *De Ira*, 1.19.4

pp. 84–5 Why . . . servant?: *De Ira*, 11.25.3

p. 85 Why . . . talking?: *De Ira*, 111.35.2

p. 85 Is . . . misbehave?: *De Ira*, 11.31.4

p. 87 There . . . dare: *Epistulae Morales*, xci.15

p. 88 Nothing . . . happen: *Epistulae Morales*, xci.4

p. 88 What . . . Fortune: *De Consolatione ad Marciam*, xi.3

p. 89 You . . . happened . . .?: *De Consolatione ad Marciam*, ix.5

p. 89 Who . . . immobile: *Naturales Quaestiones*, i.vi.11–12

p. 90 the . . . *never-ending*: *De Consolatione ad Marciam*, iv.1

p. 90 We . . . property: *De Consolatione ad Marciam*, ix.1–2

p. 90 No . . . hour: *De Consolatione ad Marciam*, x.4

p. 91 [The wise] . . . thought . . .: *De Ira*, 11.10.7

p. 91 Fortune . . . own: *Epistulae Morales*, lxxii.7

p. 91 Nothing . . . whirl: *Epistulae Morales*, xci.7

p. 91 Whatever . . . empires: *Epistulae Morales*, xcli.6

p. 91 How . . . ruins?: *Epistulae Morales*, xci.9

p. 91 We . . . die: *Epistulae Morales*, xci.12

p. 91 Mortal . . . birth: *De Consolatione ad Marciam*, XI.1

p. 91 Reckon . . . everything: *De Ira*, II.31.4

p. 92 Quotiens . . . petisti: *De Consolatione ad Marciam*, IX.3

p. 95 I . . . myself: *Epistulae Morales*, XIV.16

p. 97 You . . . hope: *Epistulae Morales*, XXIV.1

p. 97 I . . . happen: *Epistulae Morales*, XXIV.1–2

p. 97 If . . . prison?: *Epistulae Morales*, XXIV.3

p. 97 'I . . . now?': *Epistulae Morales*, XXIV.17

p. 97 The . . . good: *Epistulae Morales*, XVIII.9

p. 97 Is . . . Fortune: *Epistulae Morales*, XVIII.5–9

p. 98 Stop . . . poverty: *Vita Beata*, XXIII.1

p. 98 I . . . half: *Vita Beata*, XXV.5

p. 98 The . . . himself: *De Constantia*, V.4

p. 98 The . . . left: *Epistulae Morales*, IX.4

p. 99 The . . . tall: *Vita Beata*, XXII.2

p. 99 The . . . them: *Epistulae Morales*, IX.5

p. 99 Never . . . me: *Consolation to Helvia*, V.4

p. 102 a . . . spirit: *De Constantia*, X.3

pp. 102–3 'So . . . table': *De Constantia*, X.2

p. 103 [The . . . everything: *Epistulae Morales*, LXXXI.25

p. 103 I . . . mankind: *Epistulae Morales*, VI.7

pp. 103–4 Imagine . . . shops: *Epistulae Morales*, LVI.1–2

p. 105 All . . . within: *Epistulae Morales*, LVI.5

p. 107 When . . . destined: Bishop Hippolytus, *Refutation of All Heresies*, I.21 (quoted in A. A. Long & D. N. Sedley, *The Hellenistic Philosophers*, CUP, 1987, volume I, p. 386)

p. 108 An . . . necessity: *De Ira*, III.16.1

p. 108 When . . . philosopher: *De Tranquillitate Animi*, XIV.3

p. 110 A . . . does: *Naturales Quaestiones*, II.16

pp. 110–11 Among . . . air: *Naturales Quaestiones*, VI.31.1–2

p. 111 Winter . . . endure: *Epistulae Morales*, CVII.7–9

p. 112 Quid . . . est: *De Consolatione ad Marciam*, XI.1

Consolation for Inadequacy

Quotations taken from:
The Complete Essays, Michel de Montaigne, translated by M. A. Screech, Penguin, 1991. The notes refer firstly to the book number, then the essay number and lastly the page number.

p. 116 I . . . lettuces: II.17.741

p. 116 I . . . day: III.3.933

p. 116 splendid . . . views: III.3.933

p. 116 the . . . was: II.12.558

p. 117 strikingly . . . humour: II.10.463

p. 117 It . . . books: III.3.932

p. 118 There . . . vexation: II.12.544

pp. 118–19 Man . . . [Cicero]: II.12.544

p. 119 the . . . shit: II.37.870

p. 120 Wherever . . . equinox: II.12.534

p. 120 If . . . length: II.534

p. 120 here . . . Trebizond?: II.12.517

p. 120 Dare . . . pig?: I.14.57

p. 121 We . . . excessive: II.12.541

p. 121 To . . . blockheads: III.13.219

p. 121 Our . . . behind: III.5.1005

p. 122 When . . . unapproachable: II.12.637

p. 122 then . . . soul: II.37.865

p. 122 That . . . them: I.21.115

p. 122 most . . . disorderly: I.21.116

pp. 122–3 so . . . death: I.21.116

p. 123 [This] . . . it: III.5.994

p. 123 He . . . blindfolded: I.3.15

p. 123 The . . . being: III.13.1261

p. 124 Except . . . once: I.21.112

p. 124 admit . . . him: I.21.112

p. 125 [The . . . it: I.21.115

p. 125 to . . . offence: II.29.801

p. 125 If . . . all: I.21.115

p. 125 every . . . condition: III.2.908

p. 126 Au . . . cul: III.13.1269

p. 126 Les . . . aussi: III.13.1231

p. 127 The . . . teeth: III.5.956

p. 127 She . . . ditch: III.5.967

p. 127 old crone: III.5.967

p. 128 Had . . . naked: introductory note

p. 129 Every . . . complete: III.5.1004

p. 129 Everywhere . . . it!: III.5.992

p. 129 Of . . . disrupted: III.13.1232

p. 129 My . . . bed: III.13.1232

p. 129 When . . . wise: III.5.992

p. 130 What . . . power?: III.9.1119

p. 130 It . . . being: III.9.1121

p. 130 May . . . apart?: III.5.1010

p. 132 Once . . . clime: III.9.1114

p. 134 It . . . ours: III.13.1226

p. 135 Each . . . wonder: III.13.1226

p. 135 When . . . world': I.26.176

p. 135 They . . . sauces: I.23.123

p. 136 scrupulously . . . cords: II.12.647

p. 136 gathered . . . cloth: I.23.125

p. 136 In . . . shoulders: II.12.538

p. 138 Their . . . wives: I.31.234

p. 138 One . . . valour: I.31.239

pp. 140–41 We . . . bows: II.12.521

p. 141 Ah! . . . breeches . . .: I.31.241

p. 142 Every . . . anything!: I.31.231

p. 143 Defending . . . country: I.23.126

p. 143 The . . . nothing: II.12.558

p. 145 the . . . perspicuity: II.12.606

p. 145 that . . . itself: III.13.1220

p. 145 Anyone . . . heights: II.12.613

p. 146 In . . . fire: III.9.1110

p. 146 We . . . other: I.28.212

p. 147 What . . . found: I.28.211

p. 147 *Luy . . . image*: III.9.1112 (footnote)

p. 147 In . . . on: I.28.217

p. 148 painful . . . harm: p. 125, *Montaigne's Travel Journal*, translated by Donald M. Frame, North Point Press, 1983

p. 148 Many . . . stall: III.9.1109

p. 152 If . . . life: II.12.543

p. 152 What . . . gout . . .?: II.12.542

p. 153 I . . . etymology: II.17.749

p. 153 We . . . empty: I.25.153–4

p. 153 At . . . all: II.17.730

p. 154 If . . . tennis: I.25.156

p. 154 I . . . feet: II.12.604

p. 155 Storming . . . lives: III.2.912

p. 155 About . . . face: II.29.800

p. 155 I . . . gardening: I.20.99

p. 155 I . . . lettuces: II.17.741

p. 156 It . . . capacities: III.5.971

p. 156 I . . . her: I.21.117

p. 156 If . . . shit!': I.38.264

p. 156 The . . . being: III.13.1261

p. 157 I . . . rectors: II.12.542

p. 157 I . . . [them]: II.17.740

p. 157 I . . . interest: I.39.276

p. 157 I . . . another: II.10.459

p. 158 Difficulty . . . payment: II.12.566

p. 159 Just . . . Paris: I.26.194

p. 159 The . . . paraded: III.12.1173

p. 160 The . . . yourself: II.17.746

pp. 160–61 I . . . French: III.5.989

p. 161 I . . . them: III.5.989

p. 162 Whenever . . . *arse*: I.25.155

p. 162 In . . . everything: I.26.170

p. 163 I . . . *reputations*: II.10.458 (my italics)

p. 163 No . . . born: Seneca, *Consolation to Helvia*, xv.4

p. 164 If . . . may: III.12.1196

p. 164 In . . . spread: III.2.912

p. 164 A . . . families: III.2.912

p. 165 We . . . do: I.25.154

p. 165 Invention . . . quotation: III.12.1197

p. 166 Will . . . say?: II.10.465

p. 166 His . . . wind: II.10.464

p. 166 There . . . dearth: III.13.1212

pp. 166–7 Were . . . man: III.13.1218

p. 167 We . . . us: III.12.1175

p. 167 You . . . stuff: III.2.908

p. 167 I . . . melons: III.13.1251

p. 167 I . . . again: III.13.1252

p. 167 My . . . meals: III.13.1250

p. 167 In . . . fingers: III.13.1255

p. 167 I . . . course: III.13.1230

Consolation for a Broken Heart

Quotations taken from:

Parerga and Paralipomena, volumes I and II, Arthur Schopenhauer, translated by E. F. Payne, OUP, 1972 (abbreviated as P1 and P2)

The World as Will and Representation,

volumes I and II, Arthur
Schopenhauer, translated by E. F. J.
Payne, Dover Publications, 1966
(abbreviated as W1 and W2, followed
by page number)
Manuscript Remains (4 volumes), Arthur
Schopenhauer, edited by A. Hübscher,
Berg, 1988 (abbreviated as MR)
Gesammelte Briefe, Arthur Schopenhauer,
edited by A. Hübscher, Bonn, 1978
(abbreviated as GB)
Gespräche, Arthur Schopenhauer, edited by
A. Hübscher, Stuttgart, 1971
(abbreviated as G)
*Schopenhauer und die wilden Jahre der Philo-
sophie*, Rüdiger Safranski, Rowohlt, 1990

p. 171 We . . . nothingness: P2.XII.156
p. 171 Human . . . error: P2.XI.287
p. 171 It . . . happens: P2.XII.155
p. 171 Even . . . despair: MR4.2.121
p. 172 In . . . hand: MR4.2.36
p. 172 I . . . *nation*: Safranski, p. 74
p. 173 These . . . humans: Safranski, p. 78
p. 173 pondering . . . misery: Safranski,
p. 48
p. 174 life . . . effort: G.15
p. 174 serene . . . ever!: Safranski, p. 267
p. 174 Young . . . man: GB.267
p. 175 Sometimes . . . self-deception:
MR1.597
p. 175 A . . . monologues?: MR3.1.50
p. 175 We . . . weather: MR1.628
p. 175 I . . . me: G.239
p. 175 Only . . . sex: P2.XXVII.369
p. 176 Every . . . suffering: MR3.1.76
p. 176 If . . . me: MR3.1.26
p. 176 [I]ts . . . bedlamite: P1.3.144
p. 176 That . . . Pope: MR3.3.12
p. 176 To . . . other: MR4.7.50
p. 176 Of . . . one!: MR4.4.131
p. 176 any . . . like: GB.83
pp. 176–7 a . . . society: GB.106
p. 177 If . . . heart: MR3.1.139
p. 177 How . . . hare-hunt: MR3.4.26
p. 177 After . . . misanthropy: P1.VI.482
p. 177 I . . . me: G.58

p. 177 Life . . . illusion: P2.XI.146
p. 177 a . . . approach: Safranski, p. 419
p. 177 The . . . heart: MR4.7.25
pp. 177–8 The . . . dogs: P2.XII.153
p. 178 comically . . . gruff: G.88
p. 178 common biped: Safranski, p. 422
p. 179 I . . . on: W2.30
p. 179 the . . . people: W1.356
p. 179 Two . . . manner: Safranski, p. 427
p. 179 If . . . again: MR3.2.90
pp. 179–80 Human . . . deal: W2.243
p. 180 Not . . . form: W, preface, 1844
pp. 180–81 Our . . . how: P1.298
p. 181 the . . . fame: Safranski, p. 18
p. 181 Would . . . minds?: MR3.11.5
p. 181 suited . . . long: P2.614–26
pp. 181–2 She . . . married: G.225
p. 182 I . . . shudder: MR4.7.102
p. 182 human . . . error: P2.XI.287
p. 185 We . . . material: W2.532
p. 185 Love . . . happiness: W2.533
p. 186 Why . . . it: W2.534
p. 186 What . . . come: W2.534
p. 187 [The . . . everything: W2.210
p. 187 [It] . . . will: W2.209
p. 190 The . . . individual: W2.536
p. 190 There . . . two: W2.549
p. 191 Everyone . . . produced: W2.546
p. 191 The . . . other: W2.546
p. 191 That . . . fortune: W2.558
p. 192 Love . . . interest: W2.555
p. 192 Has . . . heard: P2.XIV.166
p. 193 It . . . badly: W2.558
p. 193 The . . . present: W2.557
p. 195 What . . . children: W2.545
p. 195 between . . . itself: W2.536
p. 196 To . . . it: W2.354
pp. 196–7 Contemplate . . . exertions:
W2.353
p. 198 There . . . *disappointment*: W2.634
p. 198 What . . . them: P1.VI.480
p. 200 The . . . life: W2.427
p. 200 'Lotte . . . you!': *The Sorrows of
Young Werther*, Goethe, translated by
Michael Hulse, Penguin, 1989, p. 115
p. 200 The . . . thousands: P2.XIX.208
p. 202 In . . . *sufferer*: W1.206

Consolation for Difficulties

Quotations taken from:

Daybreak, Friedrich Nietzsche, translated by R. J. Hollingdale, CUP, 1997 (abbreviated as D)

Ecce Homo, Friedrich Nietzsche, translated by R. J. Hollingdale, Penguin, 1979 (abbreviated as EH)

Beyond Good and Evil, Friedrich Nietzsche, translated by R. J. Hollingdale, Penguin, 1973 (abbreviated as BGE)

Human, All Too Human, Friedrich Nietzsche, translated by R. J. Hollingdale, CUP, 1996 (abbreviated as HAH)

Wanderer and His Shadow, Friedrich Nietzsche, translated by R. J. Hollingdale and collected in HAH (Ibid.), CUP, 1996 (abbreviated as WS)

Untimely Meditations, Friedrich Nietzsche, translated by R. J. Hollingdale, CUP, 1997 (abbreviated as UM)

The Anti-Christ, Friedrich Nietzsche, translated by R. J. Hollingdale and collected in *Twilight of the Idols and the Anti-Christ*, Penguin, 1990 (abbreviated as AC)

The Will to Power, Friedrich Nietzsche, translated by Walter Kaufmann & R. J. Hollingdale, Vintage, 1968 (abbreviated as WP)

The Gay Science, Friedrich Nietzsche, translated by Walter Kaufmann, Vintage, 1974 (abbreviated as GS)

Twilight of the Idols, Friedrich Nietzsche, translated by Duncan Large, OUP, 1998 (abbreviated as TI)

On the Genealogy of Morality, Friedrich Nietzsche, translated by Carol Diethe, CUP, 1996 (abbreviated as GM)

Sämtliche Briefe: Kritische Studienausgabe, Friedrich Nietzsche, 8 volumes, DTV and de Gruyter, 1975–84 (abbreviated as Letter to/from followed by day/month/year)

p. 205 cabbage-heads: EH. 3.5

p. 205 It . . . being: EH. 14.1

p. 205 I . . . holy: EH. 14.1

p. 205 Let . . . 2000: Letter to Malwida von Meysenbug, 24/9/86

p. 205 It . . . boots: EH. 3.1

p. 205 You . . . been!: BGE. 225

p. 206 To . . . vanquished: WP. 910

p. 206 the . . . given: EH. Foreword, 4

p. 206 In . . . treated: D. 381

p. 207 I . . . resignation: from *Rückblick auf meine zwei Leipziger Jahre*, III.133, *Werke*, Karl Schlechta Edition

p. 207 The . . . pleasure: Schopenhauer, W2.150

p. 207 [We . . . mental: Schopenhauer, P1.v.a.1

pp. 207–8 we . . . abstinence: Letter to his mother and sister, 5/11/65

p. 209 I . . . joy: Letter from Malwida von Meysenbug, 28/10/76

p. 209 The . . . boring: TI. x.2

p. 209 These . . . hitherto: EH. 2.10

p. 210 Would . . . side: Letter to Cosima Wagner, 19/12/76

p. 210 in . . . room: Schopenhauer, P1.v.a.1

p. 210 hidden . . . deer: GS. 283

p. 210 that . . . goose: Letter to Malwida von Meysenbug, early May 1884

p. 211 Really . . . Montaigne: Letter to his mother, 3/21/85

p. 211 gentle . . . eggs: D. 553

p. 213 magnificent: TI.ix.49

p. 213 the . . . reverence: TI. ix.51

pp. 213–14 He . . . will: TI. ix.49

p. 214 The . . . profound: Stendhal, *Voyages en France*, Pleiade, p. 365

p. 214 The . . . copulation: Montaigne, *Essays*, III.5.968

p. 214 the . . . frightened: Stendhal, *Oeuvres Intimes*, Volume I, Pleiade, p. 483

p. 214 Art . . . life: TI. ix.24

pp. 214–15 What . . . joy: GS. 12

p. 215 Examine . . . possible: GS. 19

p. 217 The . . . world: HAH. 1.163 (my italics)

pp. 217–18 He . . . mountains: EH. Foreword, 3

p. 218 We . . . sense: GM. II.24

p. 218 In . . . tomorrow: HAH. II.358

p. 218 To . . . comprehensible!: UM. III.5

p. 218 I . . . Swiss!: Letter to his mother, 19/7/70

p. 218 I . . . own: Letter to Paul Rée, end of July 1879

p. 218 This . . . myself: Letter to Peter Gast, 14/8/81

p. 219 I . . . ground: Letter to Carl von Gersdorff, 28/6/83

p. 219 How . . . books?: WS. 324

p. 223 Only . . . value: TI. I.34

p. 223 When . . . humanity: HAH. I.246

p. 224 We . . . life: Montaigne, *Essays*, III.13.1237

p. 224 If . . . manure: HAH. II.332

p. 226 Don't . . . whole: HAH. I.163

p. 227 You . . . strain: Letter to his mother, 21/7/79

p. 227 One . . . trellis: D. 560

p. 228 the . . . *sui*: TI. III.4

p. 228 good . . . things: BGE. 2

p. 228 Love . . . together: WP. 351

p. 228 The . . . life: BGE. 23

p. 229 The . . . *culture*: WP. 1025

pp. 229–30 Nothing . . . annihilation: HAH. II.220

p. 230 All . . . hurting: TI. v.I

p. 231 Dear . . . afternoon: Letter to his mother, 16/4/63

pp. 231–2 I . . . materialism: Letter to Carl von Gersdorff, 25/4/65

p. 232 Alcoholic . . . live: EH. 2.1

p. 232 How . . . intelligence!: TI. VIII.2

p. 232 Perhaps . . . Europe: GS. III.134

p. 232 I . . . suffices: EH. 2.1

pp. 232–3 If . . . together: GS. 338

p. 233 [A]ctions . . . pleasure: *Utilitarianism*, J. S. Mill, Chapter 2, paragraph 2, Penguin, 1994

p. 233 European . . . *England*: BGE. 253

p. 233 Man . . . that: TI. I.9

p. 233 All . . . derision: BGE. 225

p. 234 The . . . Vesuvius!: GS. 283

p. 235 To . . . absurdity: EH. 2.1

p. 236 He . . . pastor . . . guide: III.93. *Werke*, Karl Schlechta Edition

p. 236 I . . . depravity: AC. 62

p. 236 One . . . governor: AC. 46

p. 236 It . . . today: AC. 38

p. 237 The . . . Christianity: TI. VIII.2

p. 238 not- . . . -revenge: GM. I.14

p. 238 a . . . *accomplishment*: GM. I.13

p. 238 the . . . comfortableness: GS. 338

p. 239 the . . . antiquity: WS. 7

p. 239 one . . . philosophizing: WS. 295

p. 239 It . . . like-minded: Letter to Paul Deussen, ?/2/70

pp. 239–40 Do . . . thinking?: Letter to Mathilde Trempedach, 11/4/76

p. 240 He . . . opera: Diary, Cosima Wagner, 4/4/74

p. 240 The . . . time: Letter from Hans von Bülow, 24/7/72

p. 240 You . . . is: Letter from Hans von Bülow, 24/7/72

p. 240 For . . . woman!: Letter from Richard Wagner, 26/12/74

p. 240 Ariadne . . . you: Postcard to Cosima Wagner, ?/1/89

p. 240 Thanks . . . 'me': Letter to Franz Overbeck, late March or early April 1886

p. 240 I . . . learn!: Letter to Lou Salomé, 2/7/82

p. 241 My . . . me: Letter to Franz Overbeck, 25/12/82

p. 241 I . . . them: Letter to Franz Overbeck, ?/3/83

p. 241 scraped . . . sheep: Letter to his mother, 4/10/84

p. 242 As . . . time: Letter to Malwida von Meysenbug, 14/1/80

p. 242 Constant . . . music!: Letter to Doctor Otto Eiser, ?/1/80

p. 243 for . . . woman: HAH. I.384

p. 243 Early . . . vicious!: EH. 2.8

p. 243 no . . . *denies*: TI. IX.49

pp. 243–4 The . . . complaint: D. 52 (my italics)

p. 244 To . . . weather: EH. 14.4

Acknowledgements

I am much indebted to the following authorities for their comments on chapters of this book: Dr Robin Waterfield (for Socrates), Professor David Sedley (for Epicurus), Professor Martin Ferguson Smith (for Epicurus), Professor C. D. N. Costa (for Seneca), the Reverend Professor Michael Screech (for Montaigne), Reg Hollingdale (for Schopenhauer) and Dr Duncan Large (for Nietzsche). I am also greatly indebted to the following for their comments: John Armstrong, Harriet Braun, Michele Hutchison, Noga Arikha and Miriam Gross. I would like to thank: Simon Prosser, Lesley Shaw, Helen Fraser, Michael Lynton, Juliet Annan, Gráinne Kelly, Anna Kobryn, Caroline Dawnay, Annabel Hardman, Miriam Berkeley, Chloe Chancellor, Lisabel McDonald, Kim Witherspoon and Dan Frank.

Copyright Acknowledgements

Grateful acknowledgement is made to the following publishers for permission to reproduce extracts from previously published material:

Cambridge University Press: *Human All Too Human*, Friedrich Nietzsche, trans. R. J. Hollingdale, 1996; and *On the Genealogy of Morality*, Friedrich Nietzsche, trans. Carol Diethe, 1996; Dover Publications: *World as Will and Representation*, Arthur Schopenhauer, trans. Duncan Large, 1988; Oxford University Press: extracts reprinted from *Twilight of the Idols*, Friedrich Nietzsche, trans. Duncan Large (Oxford World's Classics, 1998), by permission of Oxford University Press; extracts reprinted from *Parerga and Paralipomena*, Arthur Schopenhauer, (volumes I and II, trans. E. F. Payne, 1974) by permission of Oxford University Press; Penguin Books: *Early Socratic Dialogues*, Plato, trans. Iain Lane, 1987; *The Last Days of Socrates*, Plato, trans. Hugh Tredennick, 1987; *Protagoras and Meno*, Plato, trans.W. K. C. Guthrie, 1987; *Dialogues and Letters*, Seneca, trans. C. D. N. Costa, 1997; *Letters from a Stoic*, Seneca, trans. Robin Campbell, 1969; *The Complete Essays*, Michel de Montaigne, trans. M. A. Screech, 1991; *Beyond Good and Evil*, Friedrich Nietzsche, trans. R. J. Hollingdale, 1996; and *Ecce Homo*, Friedrich Nietzsche, trans. R. J. Hollingdale, 1979; Random House, Inc.: extracts from *The Will to Power* by Friedrich Nietzsche, trans. Walter Kaufman and R. J. Hollingdale. Copyright © 1967 by Walter Kaufman. Extracts from *The Gay Science* by Friedrich Nietzsche, trans. Walter Kaufman. Copyright © 1974 by Random House, Inc. Reprinted by permission of Random House, Inc.

Picture Acknowledgements

The photographs in the book are used by permission and courtesy of the following:

Aarhus Kunstmuseum: 184; The Advertising Archives: 66T (DC Comics): 211R; AKG London: (Musée du Louvre, Paris/Erich Lessing) 78R, 173B (National Research and Memorial Centre for Classical German Literature, Weimar) 206, 208 (Neue Pinakothek, Munich) 212BL, 213T (University Library, Jena) 213B; Albertina, Vienna: 226L; Archivi Alinari, Florence: 234B; American School of Classical Studies at Athens: Agora Excavations: 36; The Ancient Art & Architecture Collection/© Ronald Sheridan: 94; The Art Archive: 75 (detail) 112, 126L, 141BR; Associated Press: 86R; G. Bell and Sons Ltd, from *A History of French Architecture by Sir Reginald Blomfield* (from the French *Cours d'Architecture*, 1921, J. F. Blondel & Daviler): 133B, 142T; Berkley, Miriam: 4; Bibliothèque Nationale, Paris: 5B; Bildarchiv Preussicher Kulturbesitz, Berlin: (Staatliche Museen zu Berlin – Preussicher Kulturbesitz. Kupferstichkabinet): 5ML (Staatliche Museen zu Berlin – Preussicher Kulturbesitz. Antikensammlung): 79, 171, 211L; The Anthony Blake Photo Library (Charlie Stebbings): 61L (© PFT Associates): 61R; Bridgeman Art Library: (detail, INDEX, Spain): 46TR (Galleria degli Uffizi, Florence): 80B (British Library): 84 (Musée Condé, Chantilly): 128 (Louvre, Paris/Peter Willi): 141TL (Gavin Graham Gallery, London): 141TR, 157 (Corpus Christi College, Oxford): 141BL (private collection): 229; British Architectural Library, RIBA, London: 47T; By permission of the British Library: 137 (detail) 157, 168B; © The British Museum: 14, 21, 87, 225L; Chloë Chancellor: 30; Jean-Loup Charmet, Paris: 77L; From *Cheminées à la moderne*, Paris, 1661: 142B; CORBIS: 77R, 106, 126R, 168T; Dassault Falcon Jet Corp, NJ, USA: 46TL; de Botton, Alain: 31 (*Epicurean Life*): 52T, 68, 72T, 82, 96, 99, 104, 108, 115, 116, 119, 183, 187, 193, 195, 219, 220–21, 222, 223, 234T, 235, 244; From *Encyclopédie, ou Dictionnaire, raisonné des sciences, des arts et des métiers*, ed. Denis Diderot & Jean Le Rond d'Alembert, 1751: 53; Mary Evans Picture Library: 15, 26, 198, 212BR; Flammarion, Paris, from *Les Arts Décoratifs – Les Meubles II du style Régence an style Louis XVI* by Guillaume Janneau, 1929: 49L; Werner Forman, Archive: 17B; The Fotomas Index, 154, 228; The Garden Picture Library: 71B; Germanisches Nationalmuseum, Nürnberg, 133T; The J. Paul Getty Museum, Los Angeles, California: 51; Giraudon, Paris: 5B, 225R; The Ronald Grant Archive: 40; G-SHOCK: 189; Robert Harding Picture Library: 95; © Michael Holford: 12B; The Image Bank/David W. Hamilton: 10TR; Images Colour Library: 71T; From *The Insect World*; from the French of Louis Figuier's *Les Insectes*, 1868: 197T; Ian Bavington Jones (photography): 45; Collection Kharbine-Tapabor, Paris: 197BR; Kingfisher. Illustrations from *See Inside an Ancient Greek Town*, published by Kingfisher. Reproduced with permission. Copyright © Grisewood & Dempsey Ltd, 1979, 1986. All rights reserved: 10B, 11, 33, 54; From *Brevissima Relación de la Destrucción de las Indias*, Bartolomeo Las Casas, 1552: 139, 140; Lucca State Archives: 46B; McDonald, Lisabel: 72B, 148, 188, 197BL; Patrick McDonald/Epicurean Restaurant/*Epicurean Life*: 52B; Metropolitan Museum of Art

Picture Acknowledgements

(Catherine Lorillard Wolfe Collection, Wolfe Fund 1931): 3 (detail) 38 (Harris Brisbane Dick Fund 1930): 47B; Montabella Verlag, St Moritz: 241; From *Montaigne: A Biography* by Donald M. Frame, published by Hamish Hamilton, 1965: 117; © Board of Trustees, National Gallery of Art, Washington, Andrew W. Mellon Collection: 226R; © The Trustees of the National Museum of Scotland 2000: 12T; PhotoDisc Europe Ltd/Steve Mason: 64; From *Pompeiana: The Topography, Edifices and Ornaments of Pompeii* by Sir William Gell, 1835: 83, 85; Quadrant Picture Library: 62, 88; Roger-Viollet, Paris: 17; Scala, Florence: 5T, 48, 49R, 55, 190, 201; Schopenhauer Archiv: 172, 173T, 174, 178–82; Société Internationale des Amis de Montaigne, Paris: 216; Status, Athens/CORBIS: 19; Stiftung Weimarer Klassik/Goethe-Schiller Archiv, Weimar: 231, 236; Swissair Photo Library, Zurich: 86L; The *Telegraph* Colour Library: 9, 10TL; Topham Picturepoint: 232; University of Southampton, Brian Sparkes and Linda Hall: 22, 42; Vin Mag Archiv Ltd: 66B; Agency-WCRS, Photographer – Glen Garner. Courtesy of Land Rover UK: 65; Wellcome Trust Medical Photographic Library: 230

Index

abjectness of spirit, 102, 103
abnormality, ideas about, 131, 143–4 *see also* normality, ideas about
Adam, Robert, 45
Adam brothers, 45
advertising, 67–8, 69–70 *see also* luxurious images
Aeschines, 38
Agrippina, 76, 79
alcohol/drinking, 231–3, 235, 237
Aleria, 99
Alps, 218–23
Anaxagoras, 145
Anaximander, 145
Andreas-Salomé, Lou, 240–1, **241**
anger, 82–5
animals, 119–20, 177–8, 196
animate objects, feelings of being mocked by, 100, 102–5
Antisthenes, 38
anxiety, 96–9
Anytus, 27, 37, 41
Apollodorus, 38, 39, 145
appearance, 206
Archelaus (philosopher), 14
Archelaus, King of Macedon, 32
Aristophanes, 16–17, 25, 35
Aristotle, 115, 151, 152, 153, 155, 160, 162–3, 165, 166, 207
art, 199–201, 214, 233–4 *see also* names of artists
Assyrians, 100
Athens, 3, 4, 11, 14, **15**, 15–16, 17, 21, 27, 28, 31, 32, 35, 36, 38, 41, 51, 56, 58, 67, 76, 116, 145
athletes, 33–4
Attenburg, 231
attraction, theory of, 191

Augsburg, 131, 134, 135, 145
Augustus, Emperor, 84
Austria, 131
Aztecs, 139

Babylon, 100
Baden, 131, 132, 134
Bahamas, 135
balance, 191
Basle, 117, 131, 132
    University, 208, 218, 227
beauty, different conceptions of, 136
Bellini, Giovanni, 48–9, **49**, 72
Belton House, Lincolnshire, 47
Benzoni, Girolamo, 135
Berlin, 176, 177
Beyle, Henri *see* Stendhal (Henri Beyle)
Biggin Hill, 46
Blondel, Jean-François, 47
blowing one's nose, 143
bodies, 98–9, 122–3, 125–7, 130, 185 *see also* health
Bologna, 131
Bonn University, 181, 231, **231**
books, 148, 157–64, 165–6
Bordeaux, 115, 117, 128, 146, 151, 212
boredom, 158
Bornègre, 109
Brahmanism, 179
Brancacci chapel, Florence, 201
Brazil, 136 *see also* Tupi Indians
Breslau University, 181
Britannicus, 76
broken heart, consolation for, 169–202
Buchanan, George, 151
Buddha, 172, 179
Bülow, Hans von, 240
Burckhardt, Jacob, 209

259

Index

Caesar, Julius, 117, 152, 166
Caligula, Emperor, 78, 79, 89, 94
Campania, 89
Cape Kolias, 21
Capri, 209
Castillon-la-Bataille, 127
Catherine de' Medici, **126**
Catullus, 115
Cebes, 38
Chamfort, Nicolas, 175
Charles IX, King, 128
Charmides, 35
Chelsea, 45
Chenier, André, 6
children/reproduction, 186, 187, 189–90,
    191–2, 194, 195
Christianity, 235, 236, 237–8
Chrysippus, 107, 108
Cicero, 115, 118, 119, 121, 161, 165, 166, **168**
Città di Castello, 224
Claudius, Emperor, 94
clever people, ideas about, 150–68
Collège de Guyenne, Bordeaux, 151, 152,
    153
Cologne, 242
Columbus, Christopher, 135, 138, 139
comfortableness, religion of, 233, 238
commentaries, 161, 163, 165, 166
commercialism in relation to needs, 65–7
common-sense ideas
    questioned by Socrates, 14–15, 16–20
    as societal conventions, 9–13
    and Socratic method of thinking, 23–6
    see also majority opinions/beliefs
conventions, societal, 9–13
Corsica, 79, 94, 99
Cotán, Sánchez, 46
Cotgrave, Randle, 126
courage, 18–19, 24–5, 31
Court of the Heliasts, Athens, 27, 35
Crinitus, Petrus, 115
Critias, 35
criticism, 30, 34, 163
Crito, 6, 34, 38, 39, 40
Critobulus, 38
Croesus, 101
Ctesippus, 38

cultural inadequacy, 131–49
customs, evaluating, 142–3
Cuzco, 145
Cyrus, King of Persia, 100–101, 102

Daedalus, 25
Danzig, 171
David, Jacques-Louis, 3, **3**, 6, 38, **38**, 75, **75**,
    76, 77, **112**
death, 59, 89–90, 94
Democritus, 145
Descartes, René, 180
Deuteronomy, 93, 94
dictatorship, 32, 35
Diderot, Denis, 5, 38–9
difficulties, consolation for, 203–44
Diodorus, 41
Diogenes (of Oinoanda), 67
Diogenes (philosopher), 145
Diogenes Laertius, 41, 59, 116
Dionysiac festivals, 229–30
Dionysus, theatre of, Athens, 16
Diotimus the Stoic, 51, 53
disaster, 78, 86–9
distress, 201
dog-on-leash metaphor, 107–8, 109
dogs, 177–8
Domitius, 110
Dresden, 175
dress, 10
drinking/alcohol, 231–3, 235, 237
Dufresnoy, Charles-Alphonse, 4, **5**

Eagle House School, Wimbledon, 172, **173**
earthquakes, 89, 91, 110–11
eating, process of, 123
Ecclesiastes, 118
economics, 70
education, 150–6
Egypt, 51, 154
Eiser, Otto, 240
Elephant Man, The, 40
Empedocles, 145
Engadine region, 218, 220, 222, 243
England, 172, 233
Epicurean, The (restaurant), 52, **52**
Epicurean Life (magazine), 52, **52**, 53, 68

Index

Epicurus, 50–72, 97, 116, 130, 145, 146, 160, 239
  illustration, **55**
Epigenes, 38
Erasmus, Desiderius, 115
erection, difficulties with, 124–5
Euclides, 38
Euripides, 41

facts, knowledge of, 160–1
false statements, 24–5
Farnborough, 46
farting, 122–3
Fex Valley, **222**, 222–3, **223**
Ficino, Marsilio, 116
fires, open, 133, 134, 135, 142
Florence, 4, 131, 175, 176, 201, 225, 226, 232
Florida, gulf of, 135
food, 50, 56, 58, 61–2
Fortune, 77, **87**, 87, 88, 89, 90, 91, 92, 94, **94**, 95, 98, 99
Fox, Charles James, 216
France, 115, 151, 153, 173 *see also* French, the; names of places in France
Frankfurt am Main, 177, 180, **180**, 181
freedom, 58, 66
French, the, 132, 133, 134, 142, 143
friendliness to oneself, 103–4
friendship, 56–8, 66, 146–8, 239
frustration, consolation for, 73–112
fulfilment, 205, 207, 210, 215, 223, 224, 230, 237, 243
  individuals demonstrating, 211–14

Galiani, Abbé, 211, **212**, 212, 242
Galleria dell'Accademia, Venice, 48, 72
Galleria Palatina, Florence, 4
Gard, River, 107 *see also* Pont du Gard
Garden, the, Athens, 59, 67
gardening, 227–8
Gascony, 143, 145, 164
Gast, Peter, 218
Gaul, 51, 88
Geneva, 239
Genoa, 218
Germany, 131, 132–3, 134, 142, 214, 242 *see also* names of places in Germany

Gersdorff, Carl von, 219
Giacondo, Francesco del, 225
Giordano, Luca, **78**
gods, Greek, 11
Goethe, Johann Wolfgang von, 174–5, 195, 199–200, 209, 211, **212**, 212–14, 242
Göttingen University, 174
Goulart, Simon, 144
Gouvéa, André de, 151
Great Pyramid, 154
Greece, ancient, 10–13, 115, 229–30
Grevenich, 48
grief, 89–90
Grouchy, Nicolas de, 151
Guanahani Indians, 135
Guerente, Guillaume, 151
Guevara, Antonio de, 115
Gyndes, River, 101

happiness
  acquisition lists, 45–9, 56–9, 71–2
  and Epicureans, 51, 53, 55, 56–64, 70
  Nietzsche's views on, 233
  Schopenhauer's views on, 197–8
  and Utilitarianism, 233
health, 53–4
heating systems, 132–5, 142
Hecato, 103
Hegel, Georg Wilhelm Friedrich, 176
Henri III, King, **126**
Heraclitus, 145, 163
Hermarchus, 56
Hermogenes, 38
Herodotus, 100, 209
Hippolytus, Bishop, 107
Hitler, Adolf, **211**
Høegh-Guldberg, Mrs, 183, **184**
Holland Park, 45
horticulture, 227–8
Huber, François, 196

idle opinions, 65
Idomeneus, 56
Ile de la Cité, 48
impotence, 123–5
inadequacy, consolation for, 113–68

inanimate objects, feelings of being mocked by, 100–101
Incas, 139
Indian tribes, 135, 136–8, 139–40
injustice, sense of, 93–5
Innsbruck, 131
insects, 197
intellectual inadequacy, 150–68
intellectual work, benefits of, 118
intuition, 25, 26
Ischia, 209
Isocrates, 41
Italy, 51, 87, 115, 134, 162, 175, 176, 208, 213
    see also names of places in Italy

Jena University, 181
Joubert, Laurent, 138
joy, 215
Judaea, 51
Julia Livilla, 94
justice/injustice, 93–5

Kensington, 45
Kenwood House, 45, **45**
Kirby, William, 196
knowledge, 25, 153
Købke, Christen, 183, **184**

La Boétie, Étienne de, 146–8
La Bruyère, Jean de, 209
La Rochefoucauld, François, duc de, 209
La Villa, 148
Laches, 17, 18
Lambin, Denys, 116
Lampsacus, 51
Las Casas, Bartolomeo, 139, 140
Lavallée-Poussin, Étienne de, **5**
learning, 153
Lebelski, George, 144
Leipzig University, 207, 231
Leo Africanus, 144
Leonardo da Vinci, 225
Leonteus, 56
Léry, Jean de, 135, 136, 137, 138
Les Gauchers, 119
Leu, Thomas de, 128
Leucippus, 145

Levetzow, Ulrike von, 214
Liedet, Loyset, **77**
life, ideas from, 166–8
lightning, 110
Lindau, 132
logic, 42, 141, 152
London, 45, 126, 172
Longfellow, Henry, 239
Longinus, 115
Lopez de Gomara Francisco, 135
Louis XVI, King, 6, 48
love, 185, 186, 187–8, 189, 190, 192, 194, 197–8, 199–200, 201, 214
love story, contemporary, 183–98
Lucerne, 240
Lucilius, 96–7, 103
Lucretius, 55, 68–9, 70, 115, 116, 161
Lugano, 232
Lugdunum, 78, 88–9
Luri, 99
Lusignano, Étienne (Jacques) de, 144
luxurious images, 65–7, 68
Lycon, 27, 41
Lysippus, 41, 42

majority opinions/beliefs, 20–22, 32–3 *see also* common-sense ideas
Mantinea, battle of (418 BC), 17
Marcia, 89–90, 93, 112
Mardonius, 18
Mariana, 99
Marienbad, 214
marriage, 138, 176, 192, 193, 195, 240
Masaccio, 201, **201**
Mattecoulon, Bertrand de, 131
Maximilian, Emperor, 123
Mediterranean, 209, 218
Medon, Caroline, 176
Meletus, 27, 41
Melite district, Athens, 56, 59
Mendoza, Gonçalez de, 144
Menexenus, 38
Meno, 19–20, 21
Menoeceus, 58
Messalina, Empress, 79, 94
Metilius, 89, 93, 94, 112
Metrodorus, 51, 56, 59

Index

Metropolitan Museum of Art, New York, 3
Mexico, 136, 145, 218
Meyer, Lorenz, 172
Meysenbug, Malwida von, 208, 209, 229, 242
Michelangelo Buonarroti, 225
Miggrode, Jacques de, 139
Milan, 176
Miletus, 154, 155
militarism, 12
Mill, John Stuart, 233
Minho, the, 123
mockery: feelings of being mocked, 100–105
moles, 196
money
    consolation for not having enough, 43–72
    in relation to anger, 83–4
    in relation to happiness, 59, 60–2
    in relation to virtue, 19–20, 24–5
    see also wealth
Montaigne, Françoise de (wife of Michel de Montaigne), 116
Montaigne, Léonor de (daughter of Michel de Montaigne), 116, 127
Montaigne, Michel de, 115–68, 179–80, 185, 209, 211, 212, 214, 215–16, 224, 243
    illustrations, **128, 212**
mortality, 59 see also death
mountains, 217–23
Muenster, Sébastien, 144
Musaeus, 145
Mycale, 35

Naples, 175
    Bay of, 208, **208**, 209
Napoleon Bonaparte, 200, 213, 214, 216
National Socialism, 210
nature, 110–11
Naumburg, 207, 208, 227
Nausiphanes, 50
necessities, acceptance of, 109, 111
needs, 60, 65–7
negative emotions, 227–8
Nero, Emperor, 75–6, 78, 79, 109–10, 111
neutralization, theory of, 191

New Testament, 236, 237
New York, 3
Ney, Elizabeth, 181–2, **182**
Nice, 218
Nicias, 17, 18
Nietzsche, Carl Ludwig (father of Friedrich Nietzsche), 235–6, **236**
Nietzsche, Elisabeth (sister of Friedrich Nietzsche), 210, **211**, 241, 242
Nietzsche, Franziska (mother of Friedrich Nietzsche), 208, 227, 231, 235, 241, 242
Nietzsche, Friedrich, 205–44
    illustrations, **206, 231, 241**
Nîmes, 106, 107, 173
noise, 103–5, 179
normality, ideas about, 131, 132, 135, 140–41, 145 see also abnormality, ideas about
nose, blowing one's, 143
novels, writing, 217

occupation, 54–5
Octavia, 76
Oehler, David Ernst, 235
Oinoanda, 67, 68, **68**, 69
Osann, Friedrich, 176
Overbeck, Franz, 240, 241
Ovid, 117

Padua, 131
Paestum, 209, 213, 229, **229**
pain see suffering/pain
Pamphilus, 50
Paris, 128, 212 see also Ile de la Cité
Parmenides, 145
parroting, 165
passions, 229–30
Paulina, 76, 77, 111
Pausanias, King, 18
Peloponnesian War, 17, 35, 41
penis, 124–5, 129, 136, 156
persecution, feelings of, 100–105
Persians, 12, 18, 35 see also Cyrus, King of Persia
Peru, 136
Perugia, 224
Perugino, Pietro, 224
Peyron, Pierre, **5**

Phaedo, 38, 39, 40
Phaedondas, 38
Phaenarete, 14
Pisa, 162
Piso, Calpurnius, 111
Piso, Gnaeus, governor of Syria, 102
Pitt, William, 216
Piz Corvatsch, 219, **220**, 220–21, **221**, 230, 243
Piz de la Margna, 219
Piz Lagrev, 219
Platea, battle of (479 BC), 18, 25, 35
Plato, 4, 6, 17, 19, 23, 115, 116, 122, 145, 159, 160, 161, 163, 164, 165–6, 209
Plautus, 117
pleasure, 50–51, 53, 56, 70, 233, 234
Pliny, 118
Plutarch, 41
Pnyx hill, Athens, 27
Pobles, 235
poets, 200
Pollio, Vedius, 84
Polus, 31–2
Polyaenus, 56
polygamy, 138, 176
Pompeii, 48, **48**, 78, 89, 209, 214
Pont du Gard, **106**, 106–7, 109, 173, 214
Portugal, 123, 124 *see also* Portuguese, the
Portuguese, the, 138
Postel, Guillaume, 144
pottery, **21**, 21–2, **22**, 23, **30**, 30, **31**, 31, **42**
poverty, 19, 20, 24–5, 70, 98
praemeditatio, 91
productum, 98, 99
Proverbs, 118
Pyrrho, 120
Pythagoras, 145

Quiberon, 216
quotations, use of, 161, 163

Raphael, 224–7, 232
  works, **225**, **226**
reality, 78, 80–81, 86, 107, 109
reason, 33, 82, 109, 118, 121, 145, 185
reassurance, 96
Rée, Paul, 218, 240, **241**

rejection, 194–5
religion of comfortableness, 233, 238
reproduction *see* children/reproduction
Reynolds, Sir Joshua, 6
Ribera (Jusepe), **78**
Richer, Pierre, 138
Röcken, 235, **235**
Rome, 104, **104**, 131, 145, 175
  ancient, 75, 76, 78, 79, 83, 89, 94, 99, 106–7, 110, 115, 173, 237
Royal Society of Arts, 45, **45**
Rubens, Peter Paul, **77**

Saint-Quentin, Jacques Philippe Joseph de, **5**
St Vivien, 127
Samos, 50
Santa Maria del Carmine, Florence, 201
Saunier, 48
Schaffhausen, 131
Schnepp, Margaretha, 179
scholarship, benefits of, 118
Schopenhauer, Arthur, 171–202, 207, 208, 210
  illustrations, **171**, **174**, **178**, **182**
Schopenhauer, Heinrich (father of Arthur Schopenhauer), 171, **172**, 172
Schopenhauer, Johanna (mother of Arthur Schopenhauer), 171, **172**, 173, 174, 179
Scipio Aemilianus, 161
Scipio Africanus, 161
Seneca, 75–112, 115, 117, 151, 161, 163, 164, 179
  illustrations, **75**, **77**, **78**, **79**
Seneca's Tower, Corsica, 99
Seville, 139, 145
sexual inadequacy, 122–9
shock, 86–91
Sicily, 17, 96
Siena, 131
Sils-Maria, 218, 219, **219**, **220**, 222, 243
Simmias, 38
slaves, 11
sleep, 179–80
Socrates, 3–42, 55, 76–7, 116, 135, 159
  illustrations, **3**, **5**, **14**, **79**
Socratic method for thinking, 23–6

Index

Sophocles, 118
Sophroniscus, 14
Sorrento, 208, 209, 229, 242
South America, 135–41, 142, 143
Spanish, the, 138, 139, 140
Spartans, 17, 18, 35
Spence, William, 196
sport, 33–4, 153–4
Stendhal (Henri Beyle), 209, 211, **212**, 214,
    216, 232, 234, 243
Stobeus, 115
Stoicism, 78, 98, 107–8, 130
Stoves, 132–5, 142
Suetonius, 78
suffering/pain, 194, 201–2, 205–6, 207–8,
    210, 215, 217, 224, 226, 232–3, 234
Switzerland, 131, 132, 218
Syria, 51
    governor of, 102

Tacitus, 76, 78, 144
Tautenburg forest, 240
Terence, 117, 146
Terpsion, 38
Thales, 145, 154
Themista, 56
thinking, Socratic method of, 23–6
thought, 58–9, 67
Thucydides, 209
Tigellinus, Ofonius, 110
Times, The, 177, 178
Timocrates, 51
toilet habits, 129
Trampedach, Mathilde, 239, 242–3
travel, value of, 145–6
Trudaine de la Sablière, Charles-Michel,
    6
true opinion, 25
true statements, 24–5
truth, 25–6
Tupi Indians, 136–8
Turin, 240, 242

Übermenschen, 210–11
universe, theories of the, 144–5
unpopularity, consolation for, 1–42
Upanishads, 179
Urbino, 224, 225, 226, 232
Utilitarianism, 233

Vandercruse-La Croix, 48
Varro, Marcus Terentius, 152, 153, 155
Vauvenargues, Luc de Clapiers, seigneur
    de, 209
Vaux, Cadet de, 196
Velázquez, Diego de Silva y, 46
Venice, 48, 72, 131, 175, 176
Verona, 131
Vesuvius, Mount, 209, 213, **234**, 234–5
Viana do Castelo, 123
Villa Orsetti, 46, **46**
Villa Rubinacci, 209
Villegagnon, Nicolas Durand de, 138
Virgil, 117
virtue in relation to money, 19–20, 24–5
Voltaire, François Marie Arouet de, 212

Wagner, Cosima, 208, 210, 240
Wagner, Richard, 208, 239–40
wealth, 97–8 *see also* money
Weimar, 174, 212
Weiss, Flora, 177
will-to-life, 185–6, 187, 188, 189, 190, 191,
    192, 194–5
William III, 47
Winckelmann, Johann, 229
wisdom, 129–30, 153, 155–6, 165
wishes in conflict with reality, 78, 80–81,
    107, 109
women, 12, 175, 181
writing, 148–9, 158–9, 216–17

Xanthippe, 6, 14, 39

Zeno, 107, 108